FIRST PAST THE POST®

Numerical Reasoning: Quick-Fire

Standard Format
Book 2

© 2014 ElevenPlusExams.co.uk   COPYING STRICTLY PROHIBITED

How to use this book to make the most of 11 plus exam preparation

It is important to remember that for 11 plus exams there is no national syllabus, no pass mark and no retake option. It is therefore vital that your child is fully primed to perform to the best of their ability so that they give themselves the best possible chance on the day.

Unlike similar publications, the **First Past The Post®** series uniquely assesses your child's performance on a question-by-question basis, helping to identify areas for improvement and providing suggestions for further targeted tests. By entering the unique Peer-Compare access code for this book on our website, your child's performance can be compared anonymously to that of others who have taken the same tests.

Numerical Reasoning: Quick-Fire

This collection of tests is representative of the quick-fire numerical reasoning section of contemporary multi-discipline 11 plus and Common Entrance exams, which typically have two numerical reasoning papers. One paper usually contains long-worded numerical reasoning problems and the other usually contains short, quick-fire questions more akin to traditional maths. This book provides practice for the latter question style through standard-format questions.

The suggested time for each test is based on data obtained from classroom-testing sessions held at our centre.

Never has it been more useful to learn from mistakes!

Students can improve by as much as 15%, not only by focused practice, but also by targeting any weak areas.

How to manage your child's practice

To get the most up-to-date information, visit our website, www.elevenplusexams.co.uk, the UK's largest online resource for 11 plus, with over 65,000 webpages and a forum administered by a select group of experienced moderators.

About the authors

The Eleven Plus Exams' **First Past The Post®** series has been created by a team of experienced tutors and authors from leading British universities.

Published by Technical One Ltd t/a Eleven Plus Exams

With special thanks to all the children who tested our material at the ElevenPlusExams centre in Harrow.

ISBN: 978-1-912364-31-2 (previously 978-1-908684-44-8)

Copyright © ElevenPlusExams.co.uk 2014

Second edition

All rights reserved. No part of this publication may be reproduced, stored or introduced into a retrieval system or transmitted in any form or by any means, without the prior written permission of the publisher nor may be circulated in any form of binding or cover other than the one in which it was published and without a similar condition including this condition being imposed on the subsequent publisher.

About Us

At Eleven Plus Exams, we supply high-quality 11 plus tuition for your children. Our free website at **www.elevenplusexams.co.uk** is the largest website in the UK that specifically prepares children for the 11 plus exams. We also provide online services to schools and our **First Past The Post®** range of books has been well-received by schools, tuition centres and parents.

Eleven Plus Exams is recognised as a trusted and authoritative source. We have been quoted in numerous national newspapers, including *The Telegraph*, *The Observer*, the *Daily Mail* and *The Sunday Telegraph*, as well as on national television (BBC1 and Channel 4), and BBC radio.

Our website offers a vast amount of information and advice on the 11 plus, including a moderated online forum, books, downloadable material and online services to enhance your child's chances of success. Set up in 2004, the website grew from an initial 20 webpages to more than 65,000 today, and has been visited by millions of parents. It is moderated by experts in the field, who provide support for parents both before and after the exams.

Don't forget to visit **www.elevenplusexams.co.uk** and see why we are the market's leading one-stop shop for all your 11 plus needs. You will find:

- ✓ Comprehensive quality content and advice written by 11 plus experts
- ✓ Eleven Plus Exams online shop supplying a wide range of practice books, e-papers, software and apps
- ✓ Lots of FREE practice papers to download
- ✓ Professional tuition service
- ✓ Short revision courses
- ✓ Year-long 11 plus courses
- ✓ Mock exams tailored to reflect those of the main examining bodies

Other Titles in the First Past The Post® Series
11+ Essentials Range of Books

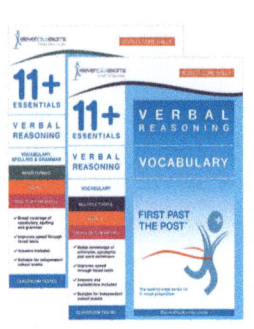

978-1-912364-60-2	Verbal Reasoning: Cloze Tests Book 1 - Mixed Format
978-1-912364-61-9	Verbal Reasoning: Cloze Tests Book 2 - Mixed Format
978-1-912364-78-7	Verbal Reasoning: Cloze Tests Book 3 - Mixed Format
978-1-912364-79-4	Verbal Reasoning: Cloze Tests Book 4 - Mixed Format
978-1-912364-62-6	Verbal Reasoning: Vocabulary Book 1 - Multiple Choice
978-1-912364-63-3	Verbal Reasoning: Vocabulary Book 2 - Multiple Choice
978-1-912364-64-0	Verbal Reasoning: Vocabulary Book 3 - Multiple Choice
978-1-912364-65-7	Verbal Reasoning: Vocabulary, Spelling and Grammar Book 1 - Multiple Choice
978-1-912364-66-4	Verbal Reasoning: Vocabulary, Spelling and Grammar Book 2 - Multiple Choice
978-1-912364-68-8	Verbal Reasoning: Vocabulary in Context Level 1
978-1-912364-69-5	Verbal Reasoning: Vocabulary in Context Level 2
978-1-912364-70-1	Verbal Reasoning: Vocabulary in Context Level 3
978-1-912364-71-8	Verbal Reasoning: Vocabulary in Context Level 4
978-1-912364-74-9	Verbal Reasoning: Vocabulary Puzzles Book 1
978-1-912364-75-6	Verbal Reasoning: Vocabulary Puzzles Book 2
978-1-912364-76-3	Verbal Reasoning: Practice Papers Book 1 - Multiple Choice

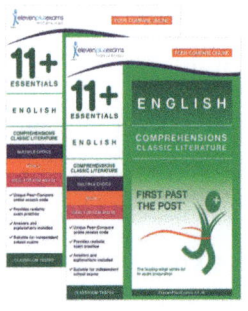

978-1-912364-02-2	English: Comprehensions Classic Literature Book 1 - Multiple Choice
978-1-912364-05-3	English: Comprehensions Contemporary Literature Book 1 - Multiple Choice
978-1-912364-08-4	English: Comprehensions Non-Fiction Book 1 - Multiple Choice
978-1-912364-14-5	English: Mini Comprehensions - Inference Book 1
978-1-912364-15-2	English: Mini Comprehensions - Inference Book 2
978-1-912364-16-9	English: Mini Comprehensions - Inference Book 3
978-1-912364-11-4	English: Mini Comprehensions - Fact-Finding Book 1
978-1-912364-12-1	English: Mini Comprehensions - Fact-Finding Book 2
978-1-912364-21-3	English: Spelling, Punctuation and Grammar Book 1
978-1-912364-00-8	English: Practice Papers Book 1 - Multiple Choice
978-1-912364-17-6	Creative Writing Examples

978-1-912364-30-5	Numerical Reasoning: Quick-Fire Book 1
978-1-912364-31-2	Numerical Reasoning: Quick-Fire Book 2
978-1-912364-32-9	Numerical Reasoning: Quick-Fire Book 1 - Multiple Choice
978-1-912364-33-6	Numerical Reasoning: Quick-Fire Book 2 - Multiple Choice
978-1-912364-34-3	Numerical Reasoning: Multi-Part Book 1
978-1-912364-35-0	Numerical Reasoning: Multi-Part Book 2
978-1-912364-36-7	Numerical Reasoning: Multi-Part Book 1 - Multiple Choice
978-1-912364-37-4	Numerical Reasoning: Multi-Part Book 2 - Multiple Choice

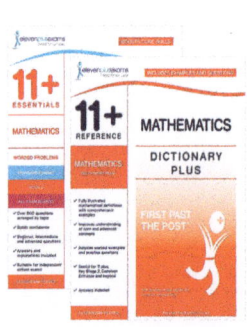

978-1-912364-43-5	Mathematics: Mental Arithmetic Book 1
978-1-912364-44-2	Mathematics: Mental Arithmetic Book 2
978-1-912364-45-9	Mathematics: Worded Problems Book 1
978-1-912364-46-6	Mathematics: Worded Problems Book 2
978-1-912364-52-7	Mathematics: Worded Problems Book 3
978-1-912364-47-3	Mathematics: Dictionary Plus
978-1-912364-50-3	Mathematics: Crossword Puzzles Book 1
978-1-912364-51-0	Mathematics: Crossword Puzzles Book 2
978-1-912364-48-0	Mathematics: Practice Papers Book 1 - Multiple Choice

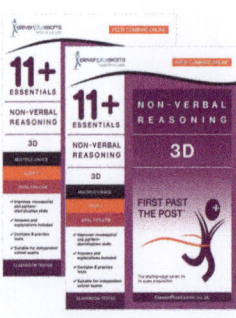

978-1-912364-87-9	Non-Verbal Reasoning: 2D Book 1 - Multiple Choice
978-1-912364-88-6	Non-Verbal Reasoning: 2D Book 2 - Multiple Choice
978-1-912364-85-5	Non-Verbal Reasoning: 3D Book 1 - Multiple Choice
978-1-912364-86-2	Non-Verbal Reasoning: 3D Book 2 - Multiple Choice
978-1-912364-83-1	Non-Verbal Reasoning: Practice Papers Book 1 - Multiple Choice

Contents

Glossary	vi
Instructions	xii
Test 1	1
Test 2	7
Test 3	13
Test 4	19
Test 5	25
Test 6	31
Test 7	37
Test 8	43
Test 9	49
Test 10	55
Answers and Explanations	61
Peer-Compare access code	inside front cover

This workbook comprises 10 tests with 20 questions in each. Each test is designed to be completed in six minutes.

Glossary

Learn the meanings of the terms listed below to expand your mathematical vocabulary.

Apothem - a line segment from the centre of a regular polygon to the midpoint of one of its sides.
Bearing - an angle given in three figures that is measured clockwise from the north direction, e.g. 025°.
BIDMAS - an acronym for **B**rackets, **I**ndices, **D**ivision and **M**ultiplication, and **A**ddition and **S**ubtraction. It is the agreed order of operations used to clarify which should be performed first in a given expression.
Bimodal - when a collection of data has two modes, e.g. in the dataset: {1, 1, 1, 2, 4, 5, 5, 5}, the two modes are 1 and 5.
Bisect - to divide into two equal parts.
Coefficient - a constant that is placed before a variable in an algebraic expression, e.g. in the term $4x$, the coefficient is 4.
Complementary angles - two angles are complementary if they add up to 90°.
Cube number - a number that can be produced by multiplying another number by itself twice, e.g. 8 (= 2 × 2 × 2).
Edge - a line segment that joins two vertices of a 2D shape, or a line segment at which two faces meet in a 3D shape.
Enlargement - a type of transformation in which the size of an object is changed, whilst the ratio of the lengths of its sides stays the same.
Equidistant - two or more points are equidistant if they are the same distance from a common point.
Face - an individual surface of a 3D shape.
Fair - free from bias or equally likely to occur.
Gallon - a unit of volume used for measuring liquids. It is equal to 8 pints, or 4.55 litres.
Gradient - a measure of the steepness of a straight line.
Highest common factor (HCF) - the largest number that is a factor of two or more given numbers, e.g. 5 is the highest common factor of 10 and 15.
Imperial units - the system of units first defined in the British Weights and Measures Act. These units are no longer officially used in Britain, e.g. inches, feet, pints etc.
Inscribe - to draw a shape within another so that their edges touch, but do not intersect.
Integer - a whole number, i.e. not a decimal or a fraction.
Isosceles trapezium - a trapezium with one line of symmetry, two pairs of equal angles and one pair of parallel sides.
Leap year - a calendar year that occurs every four years. It has 366 days, instead of 365, and includes the 29th February. The year 2012 was a leap year.
Lowest common multiple (LCM) - the smallest number that is a multiple of two or more given numbers, e.g. 6 is the lowest common multiple of 2 and 3.
Metric units - a system of units based on multiples of 10, e.g. millimetre (mm), centimetre (cm) or metre (m).
Net - a 2D pattern that can be cut out and folded to make a 3D shape.
Parallel - lines that run side-by-side, always remain the same distance apart and never intersect, even if they are extended.
Perimeter - the total distance around the outside of a 2D shape.
Perpendicular - two lines are perpendicular if they are at an angle of 90° to each other.
Polygon - a 2D shape with three or more straight sides and no curved sides, e.g. triangle, pentagon, hexagon.
Polyhedron - a 3D shape whose faces are polygons, e.g. triangular pyramid, octahedron.
Prime factor - one of a collection of prime numbers whose product is a particular number, i.e. 2 × 2 × 3 = 12, so 2, 2 and 3 are the prime factors of 12.
Prime number - an integer greater than 1 that has no factors other than 1 and itself, e.g. 2, 3, 5.
Prism - a solid 3D shape with two identical, parallel end faces that are connected by flat sides.
Pyramid - a solid 3D shape whose base is a polygon and has triangular faces that meet at a single vertex.
Quadrilateral - a 2D shape with four straight sides. Quadrilaterals are polygons.
Reflective symmetry - a shape or an object has reflective symmetry if an imaginary line can be drawn that divides the shape into two, so that one half is a reflection of the other in the imaginary line.
Regular - a regular polygon has sides of equal length.
Remainder - a number that is left over after a division.
Rotational symmetry - a shape or an object has rotational symmetry if it can be rotated, but still appears to be in the same original position, e.g. a square has rotational symmetry of four, because it can be rotated four times, but still appears the same.
Scalene - the sides of a scalene triangle are all of different lengths.
Sequence - a list of numbers or objects arranged in a particular order, which is defined by a specific rule, or set of rules.
Square number - a number that can be produced by multiplying another number by itself, e.g. 16 (= 4 × 4).
Supplementary angles - two angles are supplementary if they add up to 180°.
Triangle - a 2D shape with three straight sides. Triangles are polygons.
Triangular number - a number that can be represented by a group of equally spaced points arranged in a triangle, e.g. 1, 3, 6: • ∴ ∴·
Vertex - a point at which two or more straight lines meet.

Place Value

The numerical value of a digit in a number.

For example, in the number 1234.567, the digit 3 has a place value of tens.

1	2	3	4	.	5	6	7
thousands	hundreds	tens	units	decimal point	tenths	hundredths	thousandths

Special Numbers

	1st	2nd	3rd	4th	5th	6th	7th	8th	9th	10th	11th	12th	13th	14th	15th	16th	17th	18th	19th	20th
even	2	4	6	8	10	12	14	16	18	20	22	24	26	28	30	32	34	36	38	40
odd	1	3	5	7	9	11	13	15	17	19	21	23	25	27	29	31	33	35	37	39
square	1	4	9	16	25	36	49	64	81	100	121	144	169	196	225	256	289	324	361	400
cube	1	8	27	64	125	216	343	512	729	1000	1331	1728	2197	2744	3375	4096	4913	5832	6859	8000
triangular	1	3	6	10	15	21	28	36	45	55	66	78	91	105	120	136	153	171	190	210
prime	2	3	5	7	11	13	17	19	23	29	31	37	41	43	47	53	59	61	67	71
fibonacci	1	1	2	3	5	8	13	21	34	55	89	144	233	377	610	987	1597	2584	4181	6765

Equivalent Decimals, Fractions & Percentages

percentage	5%	10%	15%	20%	25%	30%	35%	40%	45%	50%	55%	60%	65%	70%	75%	80%	85%	90%	95%	100%	150%
fraction	$\frac{1}{20}$	$\frac{1}{10}$	$\frac{3}{20}$	$\frac{1}{5}$	$\frac{1}{4}$	$\frac{3}{10}$	$\frac{7}{20}$	$\frac{2}{5}$	$\frac{9}{20}$	$\frac{1}{2}$	$\frac{11}{20}$	$\frac{3}{5}$	$\frac{13}{20}$	$\frac{7}{10}$	$\frac{3}{4}$	$\frac{4}{5}$	$\frac{17}{20}$	$\frac{9}{10}$	$\frac{19}{20}$	$\frac{1}{1}$	$\frac{3}{2}$
decimal	0.05	0.1	0.15	0.2	0.25	0.3	0.35	0.4	0.45	0.5	0.55	0.6	0.65	0.7	0.75	0.8	0.85	0.9	0.95	1	1.5

Mathematical Symbols

+	addition
−	subtraction
×	multiplication
÷	division
±	positive or negative
=	equals sign
<	less than
>	greater than
≈	approximately equal to
≤	less than or equal to
≥	greater than or equal to
≠	not equal to
a^2	squared number
a^3	cubed number
%	per cent
$\sqrt{a}$	square root
$\sqrt[3]{a}$	cubed root
$\dot{a}$	recurring number
$a:b$	ratio
$a°$	degrees
$\bar{a}$	mean
(x, y)	coordinates
∟	right angle
$\binom{x}{y}$	column vector (column matrix)
a/b	fraction
$\{a, b\}$	dataset
π	pi

Equivalent Periods of Time

1 minute	60 seconds
1 hour	60 minutes
1 day	24 hours
1 week	7 days
1 year	12 months (365 days)
1 leap year	366 days
1 decade	10 years
1 century	100 years
1 millennium	1,000 years

Roman Numerals

When a symbol appears *after* a numerically larger symbol, their values are added. When a symbol appears *before* a numerically larger symbol, their values are subtracted.

1	I
2	II
3	III
4	IV
5	V
6	VI
7	VII
8	VIII
9	IX
10	X
20	XX
30	XXX
40	XL
50	L
60	LX
70	LXX
80	LXXX
90	XC
100	C
200	CC
300	CCC
400	CD
500	D
1,000	M

Time Conversion

24-hour clock	12-hour clock
00:00	12.00am
01:00	1.00am
02:00	2.00am
03:00	3.00am
04:00	4.00am
05:00	5.00am
06:00	6.00am
07:00	7.00am
08:00	8.00am
09:00	9.00am
10:00	10.00am
11:00	11.00am
12:00	12.00pm
13:00	1.00pm
14:00	2.00pm
15:00	3.00pm
16:00	4.00pm
17:00	5.00pm
18:00	6.00pm
19:00	7.00pm
20:00	8.00pm
21:00	9.00pm
22:00	10.00pm
23:00	11.00pm

Units of Measurement

	Metric system		Imperial system		
	Units	Conversion	Units	Conversion	Metric approximation
Mass	milligram (mg)	1mg = 0.1cg = 0.001g	ounce (oz)	1oz = $\frac{1}{16}$ lb	1oz ≈ 28g
	centigram (cg)	1cg = 10mg = 0.01g	pound (lb)	1lb = 16oz	1lb ≈ 0.45kg
	gram (g)	1g = 100cg = 0.001kg	stone (st)	1st = 14lb	1st ≈ 6kg
	kilogram (kg)	1kg = 1,000g = 0.001t			
	tonne (t)	1t = 1,000,000g = 1,000kg	ton	1 ton = 160st	1 ton ≈ 0.91 tonne
Length	millimetre (mm)	1mm = 0.1cm = 0.001m	inch (in or ")	1in = $\frac{1}{12}$ ft	1in ≈ 25mm
	centimetre (cm)	1cm = 10mm = 0.01m	foot (ft or ')	1ft = 12in	1ft ≈ 30cm
	metre (m)	1m = 100cm = 0.001km	yard (yd)	1yd = 3ft	1yd ≈ 91cm
	kilometre (km)	1km = 100,000cm = 1,000m	mile	1 mile = 1,760yd	1 mile ≈ 1.6km
Volume	millilitre (ml)	1ml = 0.1cl = 0.001l = 1cm^3	fluid ounce (fl. oz)	1fl. oz = $\frac{1}{20}$ pt	1fl. oz ≈ 28ml
	centilitre (cl)	1cl = 10ml = 0.01l = 10cm^3	pint (pt)	1pt = 20fl. oz	1pt ≈ 0.57l
	litre (l)	1l = 100cl = 0.001kl = 1,000cm^3			
	kilolitre (kl)	1kl = 1,000l = 1,000,000cm^3	gallon (gal)	1gal = 8pt	1gal ≈ 4.5l

Types of Angles

Zero angle
Equivalent to 0°
The angle AÔB is an example of a

Acute angle
An angle greater than 0°, but smaller than 90°
Angle c° (AÔB) is an example of an acute angle.

Right angle
An angle of 90°
Angle d° (AÔB) is an example of a right angle.

Obtuse angle
An angle greater than 90°, but smaller than 180°
Angle e° (AÔB) is an example of an obtuse angle.

Flat angle
An angle of 180°
The angle AÔB is an example of a flat angle.

Reflex angle
An angle greater than 180°, but smaller than 360°
Angle f° (AÔB) is an example of a reflex angle.

Full rotation
A full turn, equal to 360°

Pairs of Angles

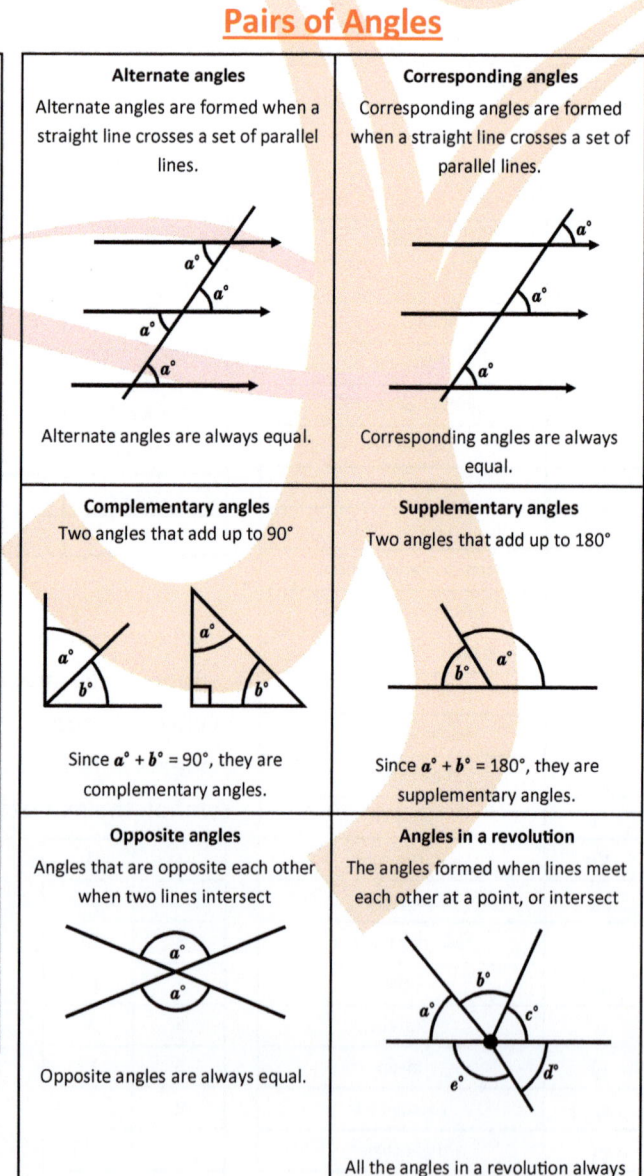

Alternate angles
Alternate angles are formed when a straight line crosses a set of parallel lines.
Alternate angles are always equal.

Corresponding angles
Corresponding angles are formed when a straight line crosses a set of parallel lines.
Corresponding angles are always equal.

Complementary angles
Two angles that add up to 90°
Since a° + b° = 90°, they are complementary angles.

Supplementary angles
Two angles that add up to 180°
Since a° + b° = 180°, they are supplementary angles.

Opposite angles
Angles that are opposite each other when two lines intersect
Opposite angles are always equal.

Angles in a revolution
The angles formed when lines meet each other at a point, or intersect
All the angles in a revolution always add up to 360°.
Here, a° + b° + c° + d° + e° = 360°.

2D Shapes

Figures with two dimensions: length and width.

Circle	Right-angled triangle	Equilateral triangle	Isosceles triangle	Scalene triangle
r = radius d = diameter The perimeter of a circle is its	One angle is a right angle (90°). The other two angles are complementary.	All three angles are equal (60°). All three sides are of equal length.	Two angles are equal. Two sides are of equal length.	No angles are equal. No sides are of equal length.
Square	**Trapezium**	**Rhombus**	**Parallelogram**	**Kite**
All four angles are equal (90°). All four sides are of equal length. The diagonals bisect each	One pair of opposite sides is parallel.	Opposite angles are equal. All sides are of equal length. The diagonals bisect each other at 90°.	Opposite angles are equal. Opposite sides are parallel and of equal length. The diagonals bisect each other.	Two of the opposite angles are equal. Two pairs of sides are of equal lengths. The diagonals intersect at
Regular pentagon	**Regular hexagon**	**Regular heptagon**	**Regular octagon**	**Regular nonagon**
All five angles are equal. All five sides are of equal length. The sum of the interior angles is 540°.	All six angles are equal. All six sides are of equal length. The sum of the interior angles is 720°.	All seven angles are equal. All seven sides are of equal length. The sum of the interior angles is 900°.	All eight angles are equal. All eight sides are of equal length. The sum of the interior angles is 1,080°.	All nine angles are equal. All nine sides are of equal length. The sum of the interior angles is 1,260°.

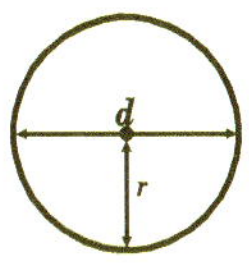

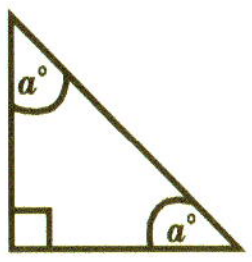

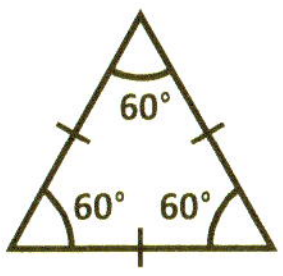

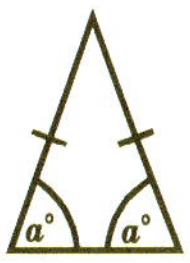

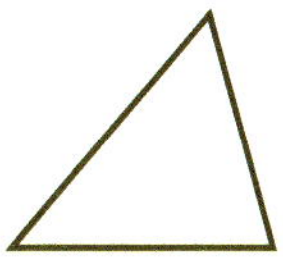

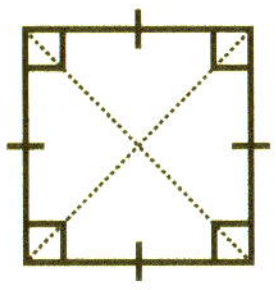

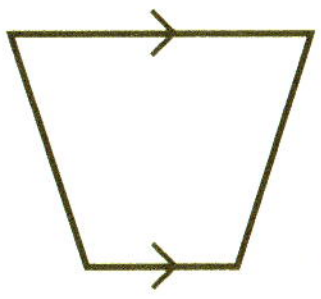

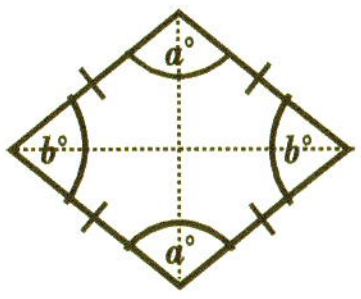

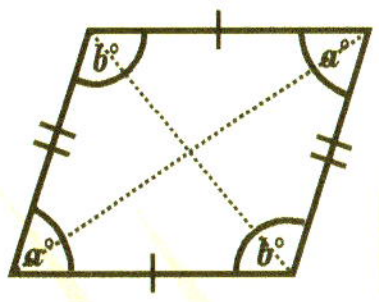

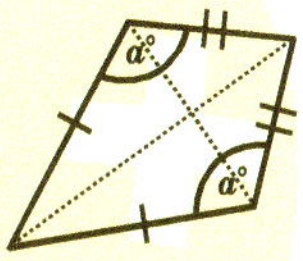

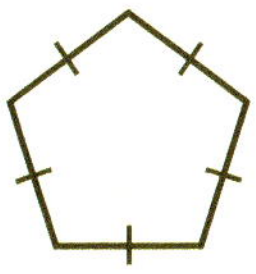

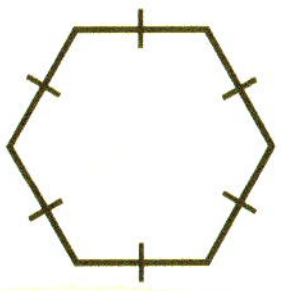

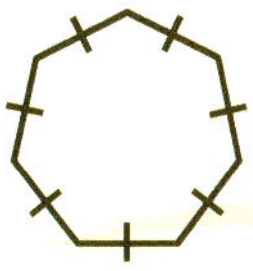

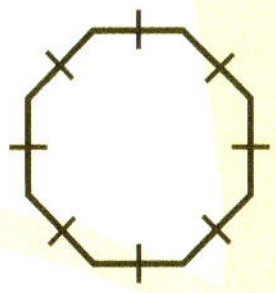

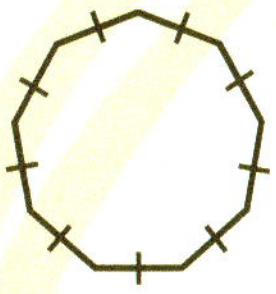

3D Shapes

Figures with three dimensions: length, width and depth.

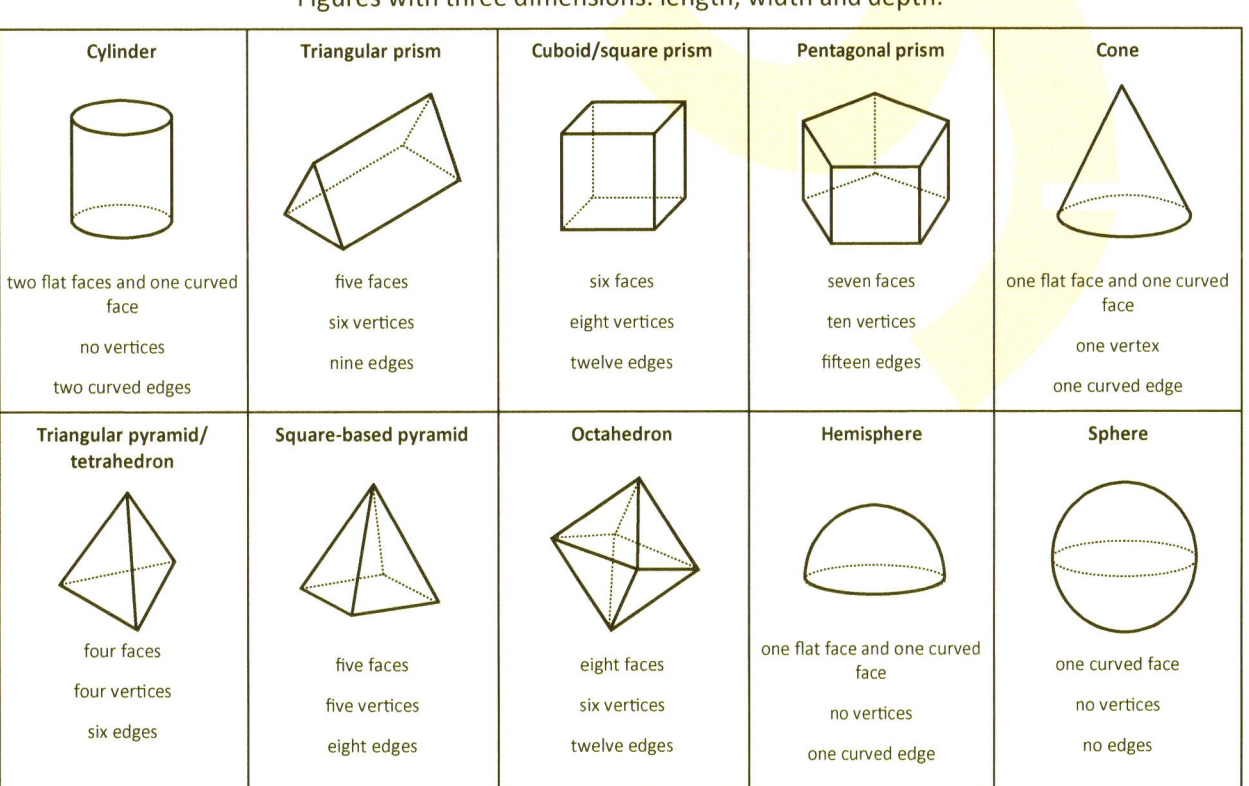

Cylinder	Triangular prism	Cuboid/square prism	Pentagonal prism	Cone
two flat faces and one curved face no vertices two curved edges	five faces six vertices nine edges	six faces eight vertices twelve edges	seven faces ten vertices fifteen edges	one flat face and one curved face one vertex one curved edge
Triangular pyramid/ tetrahedron	**Square-based pyramid**	**Octahedron**	**Hemisphere**	**Sphere**
four faces four vertices six edges	five faces five vertices eight edges	eight faces six vertices twelve edges	one flat face and one curved face no vertices one curved edge	one curved face no vertices no edges

Area Formulae

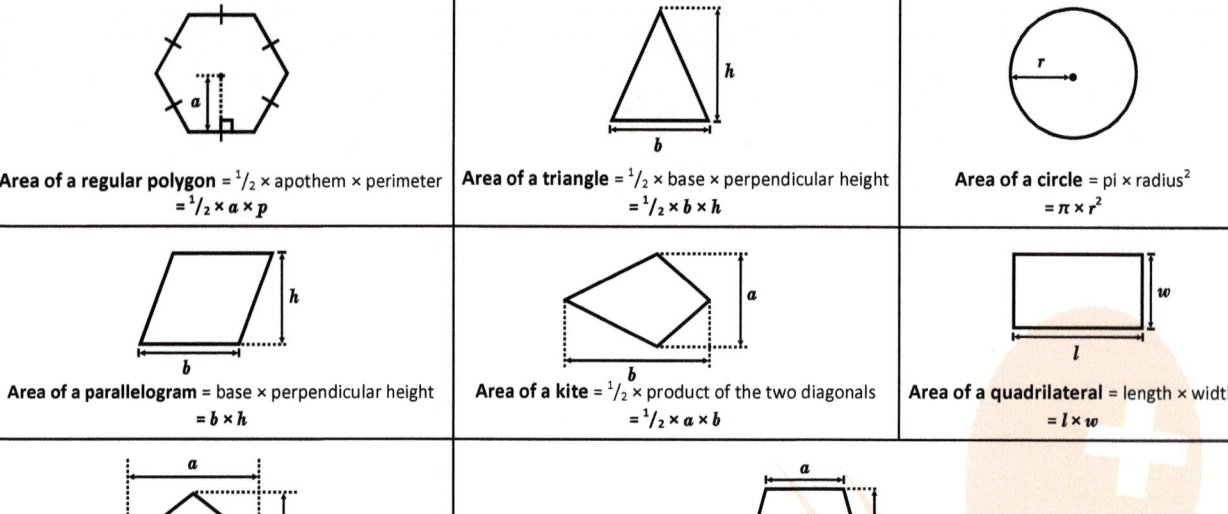

Volume Formulae

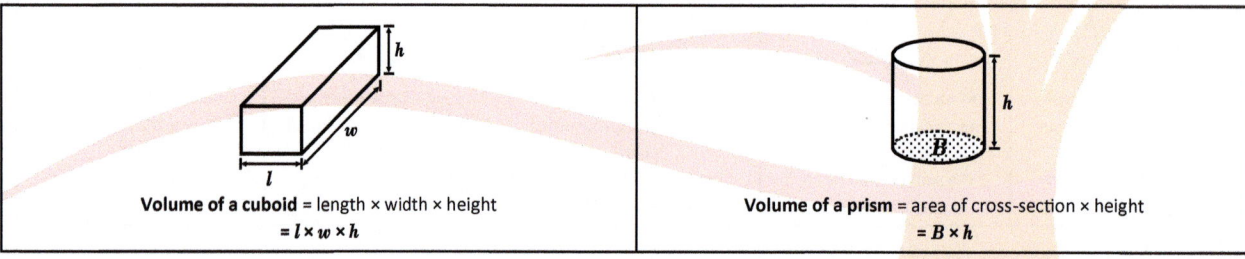

Other Useful Formulae

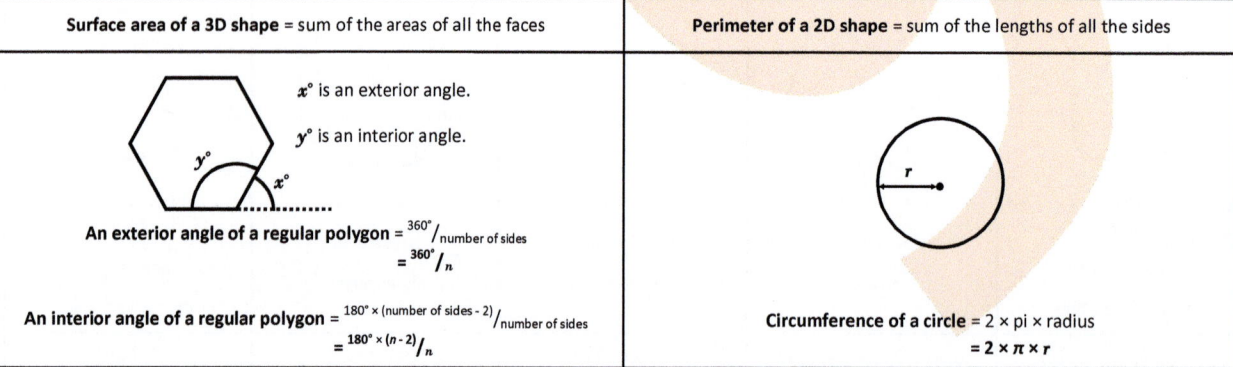

Probability

A measure of how likely it is that a particular event will occur.
The probability of event A happening, P(A), is given by: number of ways in which event A can happen ÷ total number of possible outcomes.

'And' rule	'Or' rule
The 'and' rule is used to find the probability of a combination of events occurring. The probability of events A **and** B happening is: P(A and B) = P(A) × P(B) The word 'and' is replaced by a multiplication sign.	The 'or' rule is used to find the probability of one or other event occurring. The probability of event A **or** B happening is: P(A or B) = P(A) + P(B) The word 'or' is replaced by an addition sign.

Tree diagram

One way of illustrating the probabilities of different events occurring is by using branches on a tree diagram. Each branch represents one possible event and is labelled with its probability.
e.g. a tree diagram illustrating two tosses of an unbiased coin

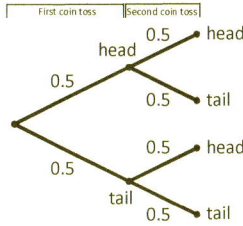

You can use the 'and' rule and the 'or' rule with the tree diagram: multiply probabilities along the branches, and add probabilities down the columns.

Probability scale

A scale that ranges from zero to one and measures the likelihood of an event occurring.

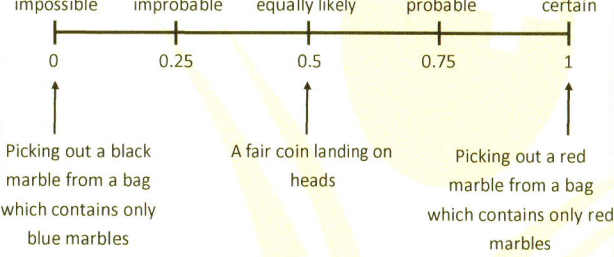

Picking out a black marble from a bag which contains only blue marbles

A fair coin landing on heads

Picking out a red marble from a bag which contains only red marbles

Remember that probabilities can be expressed as fractions, decimals or percentages.

Venn Diagrams

A diagram showing all logical relations for a collection of sets using overlapping ovals, non-overlapping ovals and a rectangular boundary.

e.g. a Venn diagram showing the first ten positive integers

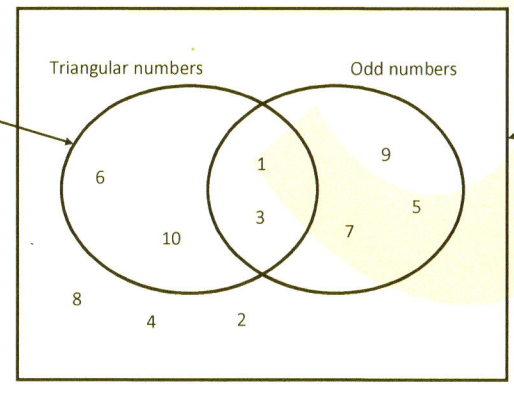

The oval represents a set. A set is a collection of numbers that share a particular property. In this case, it is a set of triangular numbers.

The rectangle represents the universal set. The universal set contains all the elements in the sets within it. In this case, it is the set of the first ten positive integers.

Some useful Venn diagram patterns:

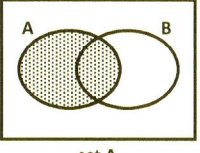
set **A**

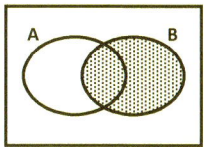
set **B**

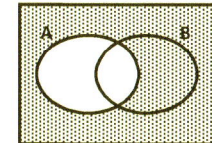
not **A**

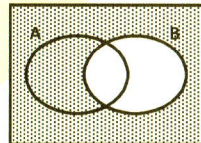
not **B**

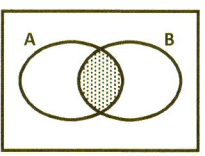

A or **B**

A and **B**

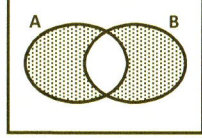
only **A** or only **B**

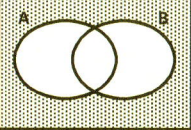
not **A** and not **B**

Instructions

Before starting each test, you will need:

1. a pencil
2. a rubber
3. a watch, clock or stopwatch

In this book, you are given boxes in which to write your answers:

Number value is determined by which box you write your numbers in, for example the correct way to write '10' is shown below:

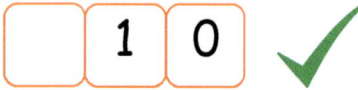   

If the answer is a negative value, use one of the answer boxes to write a negative sign, as shown below:

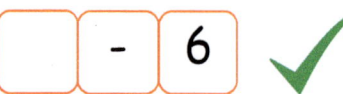   

Some questions are **multiple choice**.

When this is the case there will be a box underneath each answer for you to mark your answer.

The correct way to do so is with a **solid line through the box**, as shown below. **Do not** circle it.

Below are some **key points** to remember when attempting the tests:

i. Quick-fire questions are short individual questions which test traditional arithmetic skills.

ii. Each test comprises **20 quick-fire questions** and should take **six minutes** to complete. Therefore, it is essential that you work as quickly and carefully as you can.

iii. Calculators, rulers and protractors are **not permitted** in these tests. You should use the available space around the question to do your working.

iv. You should answer the questions in pencil. Thus, if you wish to change your original answer you will be able to rub it out.

v. If you are struggling with a question, move onto the next one to avoid wasting time. Time permitted, you can always return to any questions skipped.

Answers

To mark your work, use the 'Answers & Explanations' section at the back of this book. The mark scheme will tell you the correct answer option as well as a short explanation of why this is the case.

Question	Answer	Explanation
1	30	The highest common factor (HCF) is the largest whole number which is a factor of all the given numbers. Therefore, the HCF of 30, 60 and 150 is 30.
2	2	The lowest common multiple (LCM) is the smallest whole number which is a multiple of all the given numbers. Therefore, the LCM of 2, 3 and 6 is 6.
3	D	A prime number is a number that has only two factors; one and the number itself. Therefore, only option D, 6, is not a prime number.

BLANK PAGE

FIRST PAST THE POST

Test 1

 6 minutes

Total /20

1. What is the value of (1,000 × 0.084) ÷ 7?

2. If $12s - 5 = 31$, what is the value of s?

3. What is the missing number at the beginning of the sequence below?

| ? | 0 | 3 | 6 | 9 | 12 | 15 |

4. How many vertices does a square-based pyramid have?

5. What is the probability of selecting an ace at random from the cards shown below?

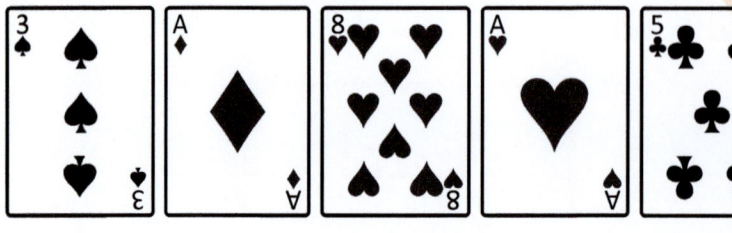

6. What is the value of the 4 in the number 8,423? Mark your answer below.

4,000   400   423   40

7. Express $5\,^3/_4$ as a decimal number.

8. Three corners of a rectangle have coordinates of (0, 0), (4, 0) and (0, 3). What are the coordinates of the fourth corner?

9. What is the area of the triangle shown? Mark your answer below.

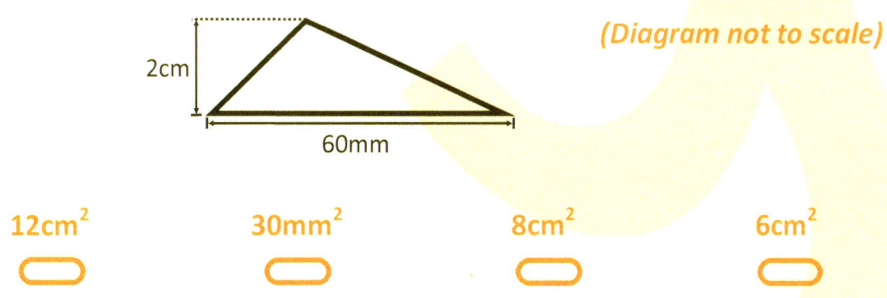

(Diagram not to scale)

$12cm^2$ $30mm^2$ $8cm^2$ $6cm^2$

10. If the input x in the number machine is six, what is the output?

11. What is the median of the set of numbers below?

    2   7   3   1   8   5

12. What is the order of rotational symmetry of a parallelogram?

13. What is the value of $(28 - 12) \times (3^2 + 1)$?

14. 600 children were asked about their favourite colour. The results are shown in the pie chart below. How many children chose the colour red?

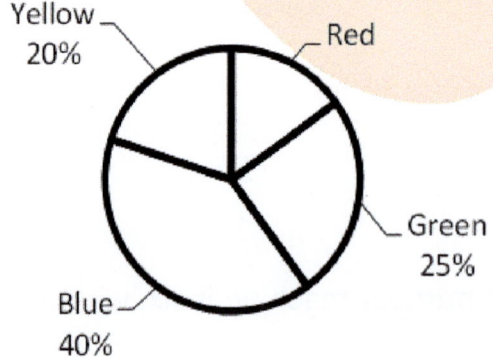

Favourite Colour of 600 Children
- Yellow 20%
- Red
- Green 25%
- Blue 40%

15. What ratio is equivalent to 48:36? Mark your answer below.

   5:4   24:12   2:3   4:3

16. What percentage of the shape is shaded?

 %

17. A plastic tube is 1m 16cm long. If it is cut in half, how long would each tube piece be?

 cm

18. What is angle $p°$ in the triangle shown below?

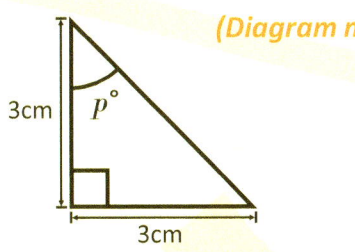

(Diagram not to scale)

 °

19. John describes the time as being 15 minutes before 4 o'clock in the afternoon. What is this time expressed in 24-hour clock notation?

20. What is the lowest common multiple (LCM) of 4 and 6?

Test 2

 6 minutes

Total

/20

1. If $y = 5(x - 2)$, what is x when $y = 5$?

2. What is 51×16?

3. Two important years in medieval history are 1066 and 1348. What is the length of this interval in years?

   years

4. The 3D shape below is a type of prism where the shaded region shown has an area of 120mm².

   (Diagram not to scale)

   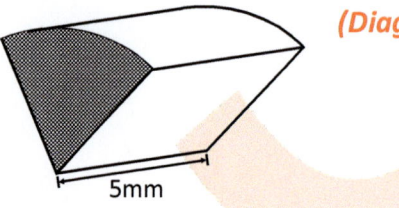

   What is the volume of the prism?

   mm³

5. The year is 1531 and the king orders that three houses and two estates are to be built in the town. A house needs 350 stone bricks and an estate needs 400 stone bricks. How many stone bricks will be required for this project?

6. Mark what the 2 is worth in the decimal number 1.0021.

2 hundreds　　　2 tenths　　　2 thousandths　　　2 units

7. What is $^9/_5 - ^1/_2$ as a mixed number?

8. Mark whether the following statement is true or false. 'The highest common factor (HCF) of 18, 32 and 40 is 4.'

true　　　false

9. How many dots will there be in the fourth term of this sequence?

10. Johan wants to round 2.718281 to three decimal places. What answer should he obtain?

11. What is 28 in Roman numerals?

12. Look at the number machine below with a missing operation in the box.

Mark the missing operation.

square root	subtract 100 from	square
input	input	input
○	○	○

13. Bella has £9.00 and this is increased by 50%. How much does Bella have now?

14. Mark the 3D shape that has two circular faces.

| cuboid | sphere | cylinder | pyramid |
| ○ | ○ | ○ | ○ |

15. The ratio of the number of physics, chemistry and biology books in a bookshop is 5:4:3. If there are 132 books in total, how many are chemistry books?

16. What is the range of the spelling test scores below?

17. What is the probability of selecting a red ball from a bag containing five red balls and nine blue balls?

18. Look at the measurement indicated by the arrow below.

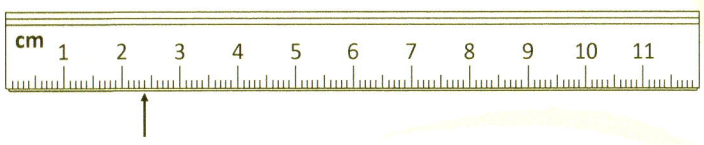

What is this length in millimetres?

 mm

19. Given that two angles in a triangle are 42° and 91°, what is the third angle?

 °

20. Consider the shape below which consists of a square and a triangle.

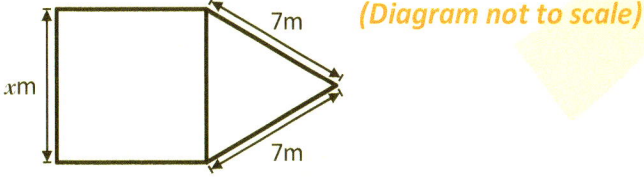

(Diagram not to scale)

Mark the expression for the perimeter of the shape in metres.

$3(x + 7)$ $3x + 14$ $3x + 7$

BLANK PAGE

FIRST PAST THE POST

Test 3

 6 minutes

Total /20

1. Yasmine buys a clock for £8.40 and a hand towel for £3.75. If she pays with a £20 note, how much change does she receive?

£

2. What is the reading on the weighing scales below?

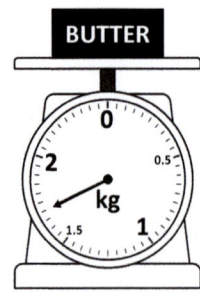

 kg

3. What is the result of $5^3 + 2^2$ expressed in Roman numerals?

4. John adds the fractions $^5/_6$ and $^5/_{12}$ and expresses his simplified answer as a mixed number. Mark the correct answer below.

　　$2\,^3/_4$　　　　$1\,^1/_8$　　　　$1\,^1/_4$　　　　$1\,^1/_6$
　　　◯　　　　　　◯　　　　　　◯　　　　　　◯

5. Flavia is facing northwest (NW). She turns clockwise through 225°. Which direction is Flavia now facing?

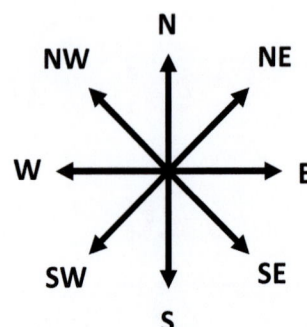

6. In total, how many pairs of parallel sides are there on all the 2D shapes listed below?

   parallelogram   regular pentagon   regular hexagon   square

   kite   trapezium   triangle

7. What is the volume of the wedge shape shown below?

   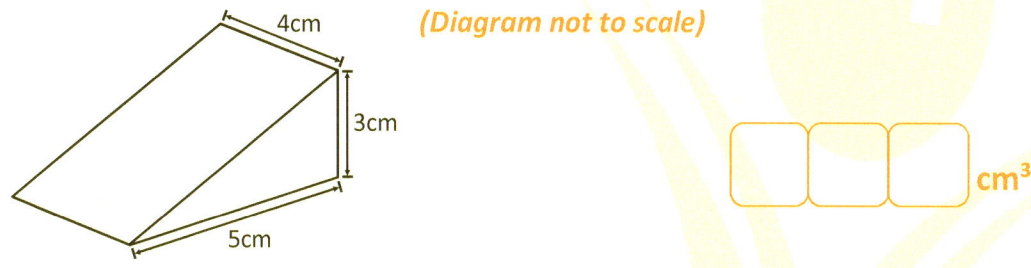

   (Diagram not to scale)

   cm³

8. Point P has coordinates (-2, 2). What would be the new coordinates of P after it has been rotated 90° clockwise about the origin (0, 0)?

   (☐☐ , ☐☐)

9. What is the order of rotational symmetry of a rhombus?

10. The Venn diagram below shows how many children attend an athletics club (A) and a karate club (K) at school. How many children belong to the karate club?

11. What are the factors of 15? Mark your answer below.

      3, 5, 10, 15 ◯   1, 3, 5, 10 ◯   1, 3, 5, 15 ◯   2, 3, 5, 15 ◯

12. What is the mean of the set of numbers below?

      1   4   3   1   4   5

☐☐.☐☐

13. How much water is in the container below?

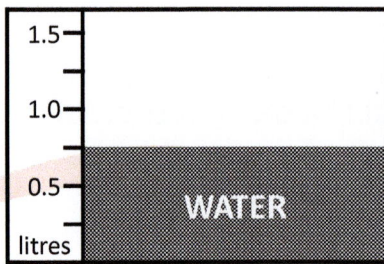

☐☐☐☐.☐☐ ml

14. In a particular leap year, 25th February is a Friday. On which day of the week would the third day of the following month fall? Mark your answer below.

Monday ◯   Tuesday ◯   Wednesday ◯   Thursday ◯   Friday ◯   Saturday ◯   Sunday ◯

15. One side of a regular nonagon measures 14mm. What is the perimeter of the shape expressed in centimetres (cm)?

☐☐☐.☐☐ cm

16. Rohit answered all 50 questions in his maths test and scored 60%. How many questions did Rohit get right?

17. What is the probability of scoring a double three when two six-sided fair dice are rolled?

18. If $r = 7$, $s = 4$ and $t = 2$, what is $(r + s) \times (r - t)$?

19. The net below forms a cube when folded. Which square will form the top of the cube?

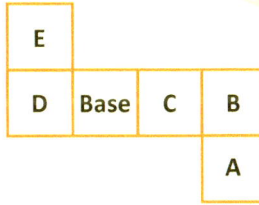

20. What number should replace the question mark in the sequence below?

| 49 | 36 | 25 | ? | 9 | 4 | 1 |

BLANK PAGE

FIRST PAST THE POST

Test 4

 6 minutes

Total

/20

1. The chart below shows the number of episodes in a TV show over its first six seasons.

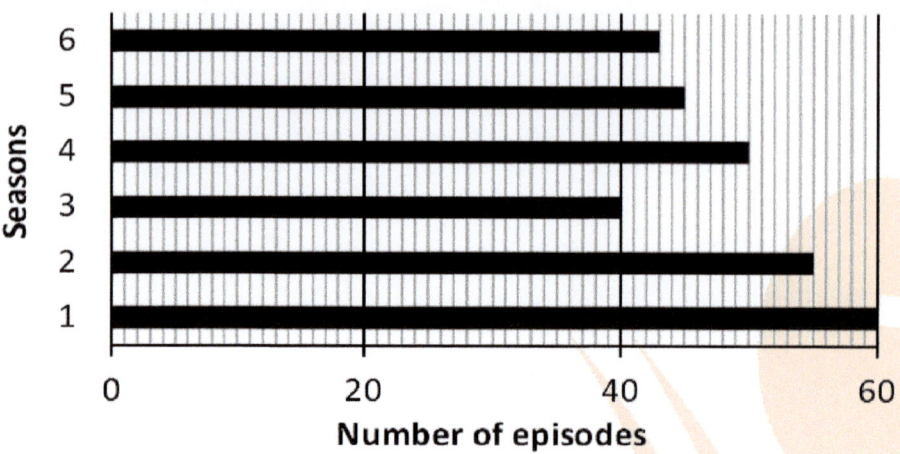

How many episodes were there in total during the six seasons?

2. What is 13 - (5 × 1 ÷ 5)?

3. Calculate $4^3 - 3^3$.

4. How many sides does a decagon have?

5. What are the prime factors of 100? Mark your answer below.

1, 2, 2, 5, 10	2, 2, 3, 5	2, 2, 5, 5	1, 2, 5, 5
○	○	○	○

6. Express 300 ÷ 160 as an improper fraction in its lowest terms.

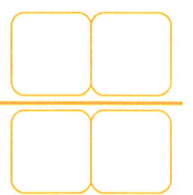

7. How many lines of symmetry does the shape below have?

8. A sequence starts n, $2n$, $3n$ and so on. If the sum of the first four terms is 70, what is the value of n?

9. What are the underlined digits worth in the number 2,00<u>0</u>? Mark your answer below.

2 thousands 0 hundreds	2 thousands 0 units	2 hundreds 0 tens	2 units 0 thousands
○	○	○	○

10. Two coordinates on a line are A (0, 0) and B (6, 6). What are the coordinates of the midpoint of the line AB?

11. Mark the event below which is impossible.

It will rain for two days in London. ⬭

An earthquake will occur somewhere in the world. ⬭

A car's speed will exceed 10,000mph. ⬭

12. What is the value of (9 × 12) ÷ 4?

13. The final position of the shape ABCD after a clockwise rotation of 270° about point D is shown on the graph below. What were the coordinates of corner B when the shape was in its original position?

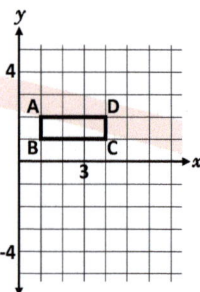

14. A lift can hold a total weight of 1,680kg. If the average weight of a person is 80kg, what is the maximum number of people the lift can hold?

15. What is the volume of a square-based column when the length of the base is 40cm and the height of the column is 5m? Give your answer in m³.

 m³

16. Solve the equation below and hence mark the value of p.

$$3 \times 2p + 8 = 4p$$

-4 ◯   24 ◯   -24 ◯   -12 ◯   8 ◯

17. Consider the word **ANTITHESIS**. What percentage of the letters are consonants?

☐☐☐ %

18. What is the value of 1.2 - (44 ÷ 100)?

☐☐.☐☐

19. What are the combined number of vertices of a cuboid and a tetrahedron?

☐☐

20. What time in the evening is indicated on Theo's clock below? Express your answer in 24-hour clock format.

☐☐:☐☐

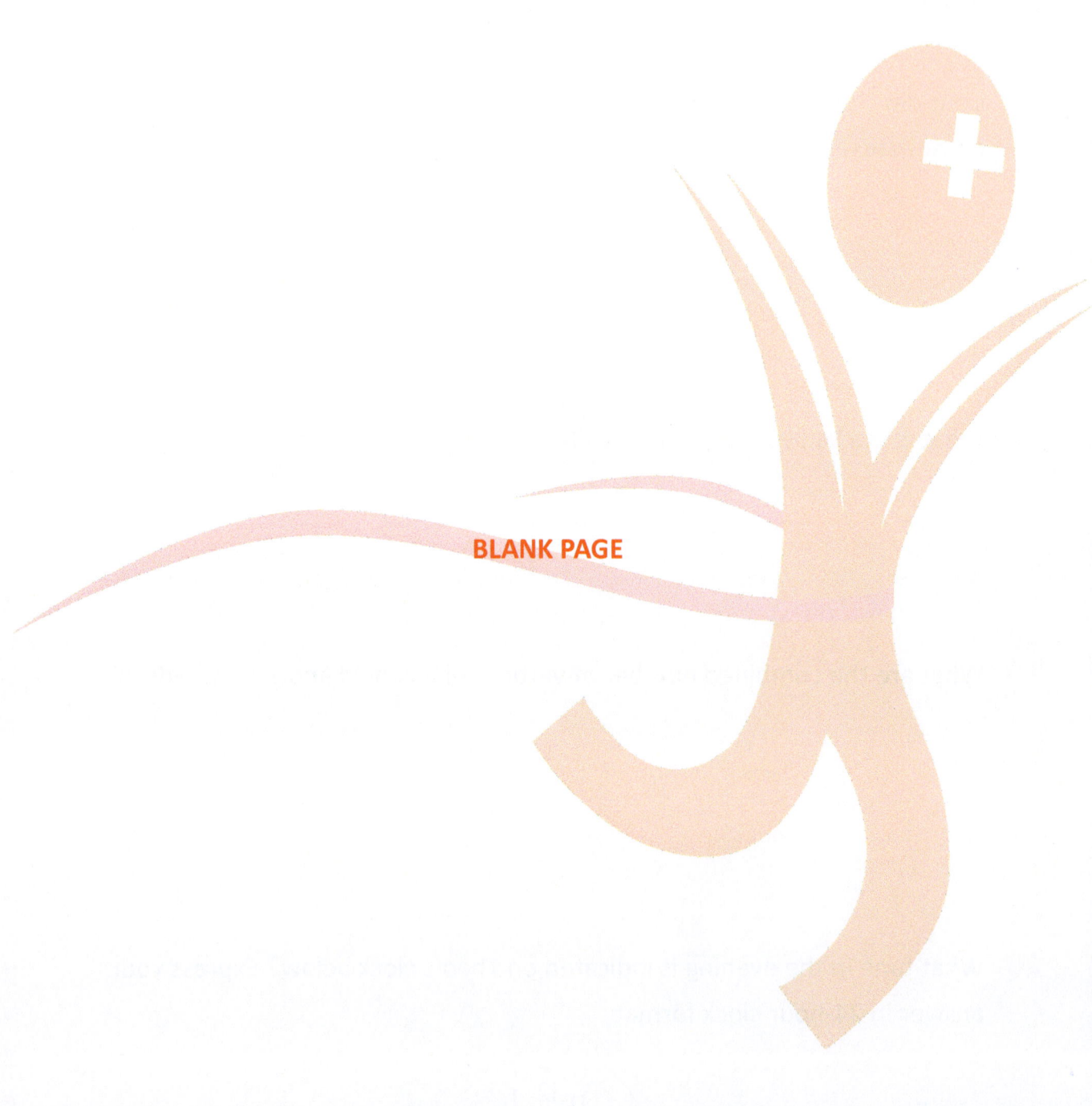

FIRST PAST THE POST

Test 5

6 minutes

Total

/20

1. Round 57,083 to the nearest 100.

2. The pictogram below shows the number of houses sold by an estate agent in a four-month period. How many houses were sold in total in the months of July and August?

3. Convert $1m^2$ into cm^2. Mark your answer below.

$1,000cm^2$ $100cm^2$ $10,000cm^2$ $100,000cm^2$

4. Carla bought 11 items for £2.05 each and 4 items for £1.05 each. How much did Carla spend altogether?

5. The plan view of a fair spinner is shown below. What is the probability that it lands on a white area?

black
grey
white

6. Andy used the rule 'subtract 2 and then multiply by 3' to find each term from the previous term in the following sequence: 4, 6, 12, 30, … . What is the next term in the sequence?

7. What is the missing input in the number machine shown below?

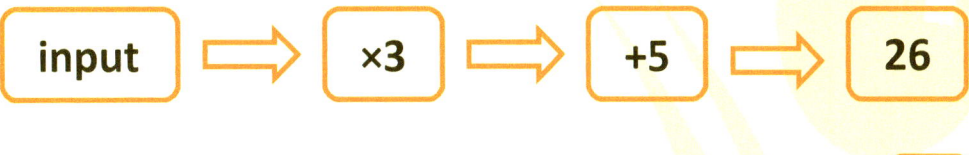

8. The cost of hiring a coach is £50 plus £3 for every mile travelled. Mark the expression below for the cost in £ of a journey of d miles.

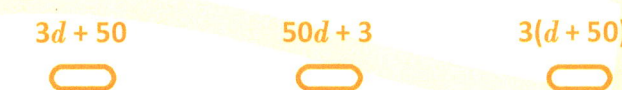

9. The bottom-end coordinates of a vertical line are (5, 3). Mark below the possible coordinates for the top end of the line.

10. What is the measurement in millimetres (mm) indicated by the arrow on the ruler below?

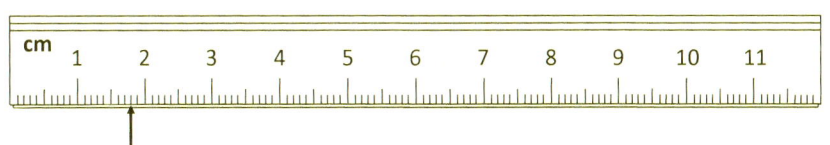

mm

11. Tanya has 84 counters in a bag. 3 in every 4 counters are blue. How many counters in Tanya's bag are **not** blue?

12. A carpenter charges a fixed call-out charge and a cost per hour of work as shown on the graph. What is the total charge for a job which takes five hours?

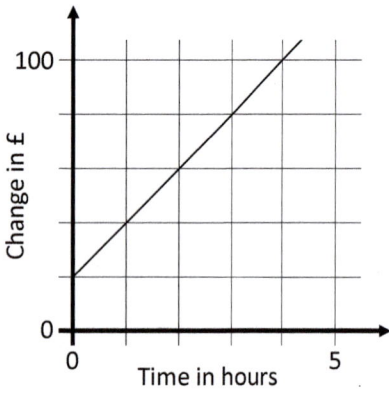

£

13. A cube has a volume of 64cm^3. What is the width of the cube?

 cm

14. The top-left corner of a square has coordinates (0, 2). What are the new coordinates of the same corner when the square is translated five units to the right and one unit down?

15. Okello adds up the number of edges on shapes A and B below and subtracts the number of edges on Shape C from the result. What answer should Okello get?

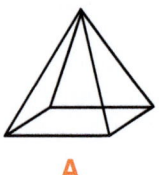 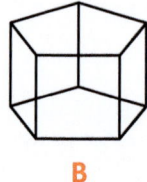 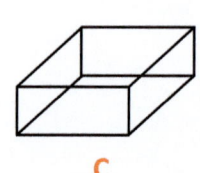
A   B   C

16. What is the mode of the set of numbers below?

8   0   4   12   6   1   8   4   0   9   4

17. Which two lines are at right angles to each other? Mark your answer below.

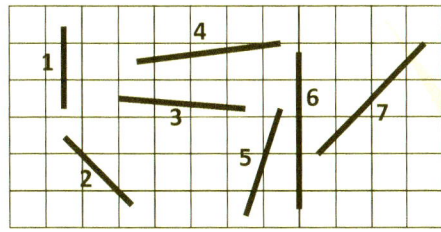

 and ☐

18. 40% of the 25 children in Kim's class are girls. How many boys are in the class?

19. The pool surround, ABCD, has the measurements shown on the diagram below. The pool, EFGH, is set 1m inside the surround on all sides. What is the area of the pool?

(Diagram not to scale)

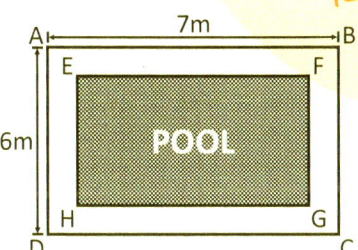

 m²

20. A 2D shape has two pairs of adjacent equal sides, one pair of equal angles, no rotational symmetry and one line of symmetry. Mark the shape below that fits this description.

rhombus   rectangle   kite   triangle
   ○   ○   ○   ○

FIRST PAST THE POST

Test 6

 6 minutes

Total /20

1. Rose has a shuffled set of 18 cards with one number written on each. The numbers on the cards are the first 6 square numbers, the first 6 triangular numbers and the numbers 5, 10, 15, 20, 25 and 30. Rose selects a card at random from the set, what is the probability the number on the card is divisible by 10?

2. Look at the two triangles on the grid below. What are the coordinates of the corners P and Q?

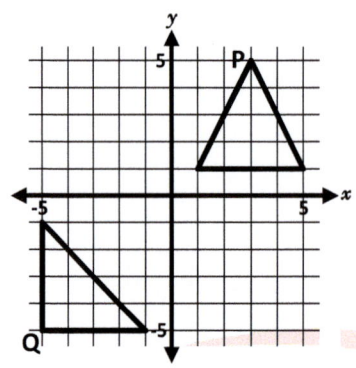

3. Varun wants to work out the value of 720 - (169 + 234 + 78). What should his answer be?

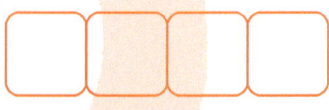

4. A quantity of 250 apples are split into four piles in the ratio 1:2:2:5. How many apples will be in the largest pile?

5. Write 'two million nine thousand and four point seven' as a number.

6. Amelie's height is 178.5cm and her sister Sophie's height is 153.7cm. What is the difference in their heights in millimetres?

 mm

7. A door is open at an angle of 144° from its door frame. Mark the type of angle this is below.

8. The diagram below shows a side view of a swimming pool.

(Diagram not to scale)

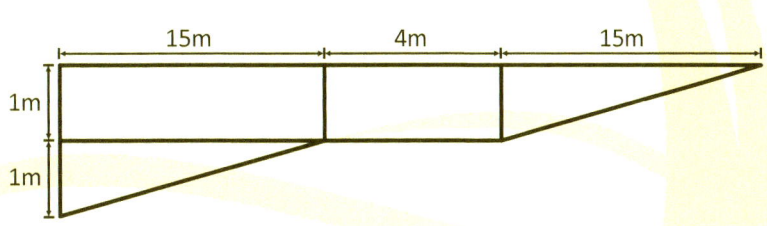

Calculate the total area of this shape.

 m²

9. Consider the equation below.

$$11^2 - x = 4^3$$

What is the value of x?

10. What is 468 ÷ 4? Round your answer to the nearest 10.

11. A sequence starts 64, 16, 4, 1, $^1/_4$, ... Mark the next two terms of this sequence.

$^1/_{16}$ and $^1/_{64}$ $^1/_2$ and $^1/_{32}$ $^1/_8$ and $^1/_{24}$

12. What is the median of the first six prime numbers?

13. A number machine has an input of t and an instruction to multiply the input by 0.7. Given that $t = 20$, what is the output?

14. What is the product of the number of sides on a triangle, an octagon and a nonagon?

15. Postman Phil delivers letters and parcels along several streets according to the timetable.

Street	Arrival Times
Sailor Street	07:30
West Way	08:15
Sigmund Street	08:29
Rascals Road	09:29

What is the interval (in minutes) between arriving at West Way and arriving at Rascals Road?

 minutes

16. An internet website has 5,000 visitors in one day. 88% of the visitors said they liked the website and 5% disliked it. How many visitors neither liked nor disliked the website per day?

17. Point P (-4, 3) undergoes a reflection in the x-axis and then a translation 10 units to the right. What are the new coordinates of P?

18. The capacity of a cuboid-shaped tank is 150 litres and it is full of liquid helium. A leak occurs and the tank's level is reduced by a third. Work out how much is left in the tank in millilitres (ml).

19. What is the order of rotational symmetry of an equilateral triangle?

20. Express p in terms of q and r in the equation below.

$$2(p + 3q) = r$$

Mark the correct answer.

$p = r - (^3/_2)q$ $p = ^r/_2 - 3q$ $p = 2r - 3q$

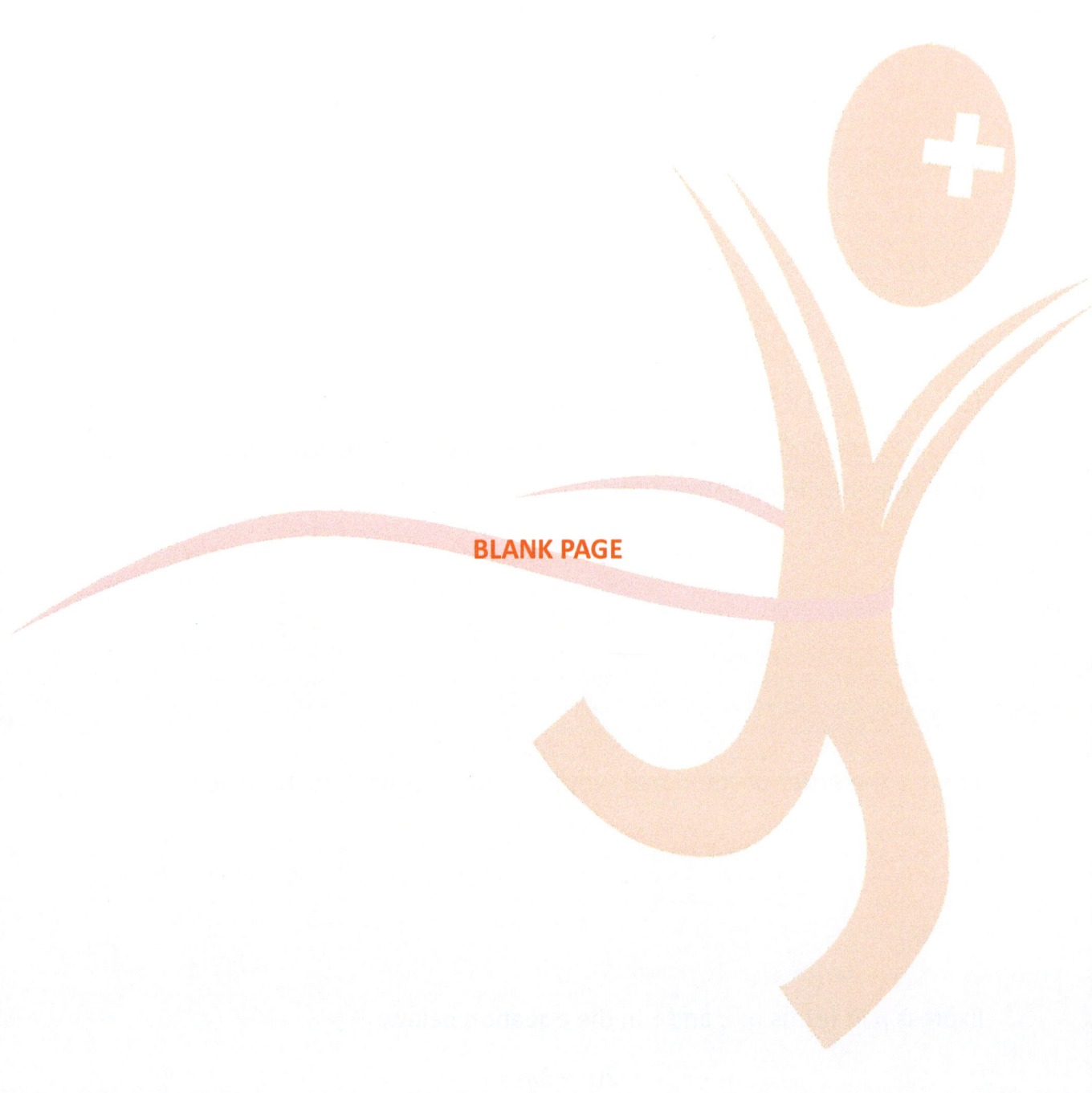

FIRST PAST THE POST

Test 7

   6 minutes

Total /20

1. Ajani buys nine identical pencils for £1.62. His friend Pippa buys only seven of the same pencils. How much did Pippa have to pay?

   £ ☐☐ . ☐☐

2. What is $^{37}/_8$ expressed as a mixed number? Mark your answer below.

   $4\,^5/_8$ ⚪ $5\,^3/_8$ ⚪ $3\,^7/_8$ ⚪ $4\,^1/_4$ ⚪

3. What is the input to the number machine shown below?

   input ⇒ ÷7 ⇒ 12

   ☐☐

4. What number should replace a in the expression below?

   $$28 - 11 + 9 = 14 + 37 - a$$

   ☐☐

5. Round 439,728 to the nearest 10,000.

   ☐☐☐☐☐☐

6. Fabia subtracts the highest common factor (HCF) of 30, 60 and 75 from the lowest common multiple (LCM) of 9, 12 and 18. What should Fabia's answer be?

7. The table below has been created from the equation $y = 4x - 3$. What number will replace the question mark in the table?

x	3	?	0
y	9	25	-3

8. What is the positive square root of $(3^2 + 4^2)$?

9. In total, how many circles are required to complete the next two terms in the sequence?

   ? ?

10. What is 0.4 × 0.4 × 0.4?

11. What speed (in km per hour) is shown in the distance-time graph below?

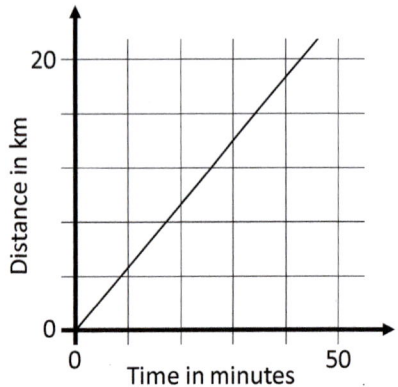

 km per hour

12. A square has a width of 100mm. What is the radius (in cm) of the largest circle that can be drawn inside the square?

 cm

13. What is the value of angle $n°$ in the diagram below?

(Diagram not to scale)

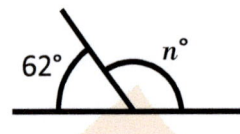

 °

14. If a fair six-sided die is rolled, what is the probability of scoring a two or more?

15. £360 is shared in the ratio 3:2. What is the difference between the larger share and the smaller share?

16. Kai purchased twenty-eight 20cm-by-20cm tiles to cover a 1m-by-1m wall area. How many tiles will be left over after the tiling is complete?

17. Nishi wants to make a 3D square-based pyramid out of paper. What 2D shapes will make up the net? Mark your answer below.

1 square
3 triangles

2 squares
4 triangles

1 square
4 triangles

18. A 2D shape has four corners ABCD at coordinates A (1, 4), B (10, 4), C (9, 0), D (0, 0). What 2D shape is it? Mark your answer below.

square   rectangle   rhombus   parallelogram

19. A part of a regular shape with two of its dashed lines of symmetry is shown below. What is the perimeter of the complete shape?

(Diagram not to scale)

6mm

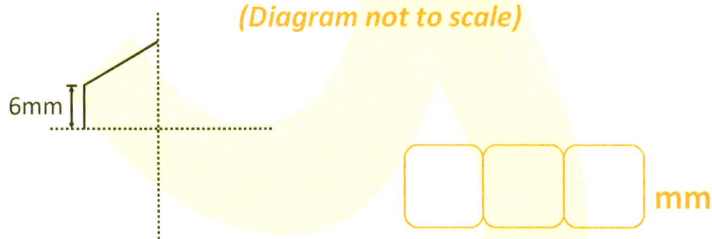 mm

20. Dario is waiting at the High Street stop at 08:50 for a bus to take him to the library stop. What is the earliest time he can arrive at the library stop by bus?

Stops	Bus A	Bus B
Depot	08:30	08:45
High Street	08:40	08:55
Museum	08:45	09:00
Station	08:53	09:08
Library	09:00	09:15
Hospital	09:08	09:23

☐☐ : ☐☐

BLANK PAGE

Test 8

Total /20

1. There are 50 identical balls in a box. If three are added and four are taken away from the box every hour, how many hours will you have to wait until there are no balls left?

2. The thermometers below show the temperatures in two locations. What is the difference between the temperatures of these locations?

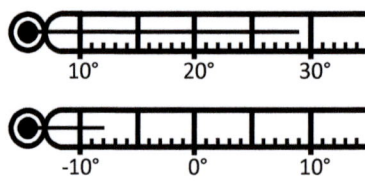

 °C

3. A and B are independent events. The probability of event A happening is $^3/_{10}$ and the probability of event B happening is q. If the probability of events A and B both occurring is $^3/_{20}$, what is the value of q?

4. The volume of a cube is 27mm³. What is the length of one of its sides?

 mm

5. The measuring jug contains fruit juice. Write the amount of fruit juice in the jug in millilitres.

ml

6. What is the highest common factor (HCF) of 20, 44 and 64?

7. What is the value of $1\frac{1}{4} - \frac{9}{10}$?

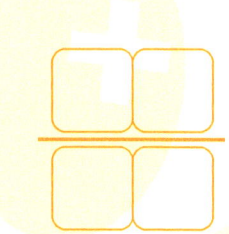

8. Point P (x, y) is a corner of a rectangle. Corner Q is directly above P and corner R lies on the same horizontal line as P. PQ is 3 units long and PR is 4 units long. Mark the possible coordinates of Q and R in terms of x and y.

Q $(x + 3, y)$	Q $(x + 4, y + 3)$	Q $(4x, 3y)$	Q $(x, y + 3)$
R $(x, y + 4)$	R $(0, 0)$	R $(x + 4, y + 3)$	R $(x + 4, y)$
○	○	○	○

9. For the following set of numbers, mark the statement that is true.

9   18   7   15   16

mean > median   mean < median   mean = median
      ○   ○   ○

10. In the parallelogram below, what is the size of the angle marked $a°$?

(Diagram not to scale)

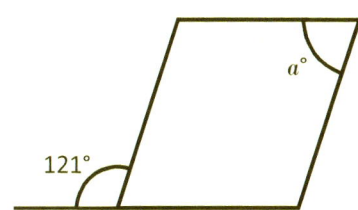

11. What is the value of the question mark in the equation below?

    987 - ? = 519

12. Determine the value of a when v = 4500 and b = 10 in the formula below.

    $v = a(1000 - b^2)$

13. The pie chart below shows the types of musical organs made by a factory. Mark the type of organ that represents 25% of the total number made.

    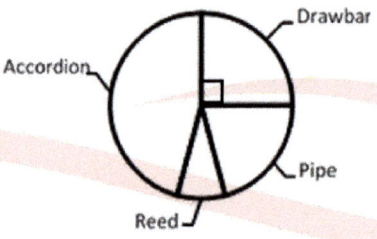

    accordion   drawbar   pipe   reed

14. What must the value of the output in a number machine be when the instruction is to multiply the input by zero?

15. An irregular pentagon has side lengths 3.7cm, 2.4cm, 2.1cm, 3.5cm and 2.8cm. What is the perimeter of the pentagon?

     cm

16. Mark the 3D shape below that has an odd number of faces.

    tetrahedron   cube   pentagonal prism   cone

17. Roxanne's birthday is on the 27th of August and Rhonda's birthday is on the 10th of October. How many days separate these dates?

18. How many lines of symmetry does the capital letter '**H**' have?

19. The square below shows a scaled-down plan of a car park:

(Diagram not to scale)

4cm

The ratio for side length between the plan and the actual car park is 1cm:25m. What is the side length of the car park in kilometres?

☐☐☐.☐ km

20. Mark the shape that has three pairs of parallel sides.

    trapezium   triangle   regular hexagon   kite   regular heptagon

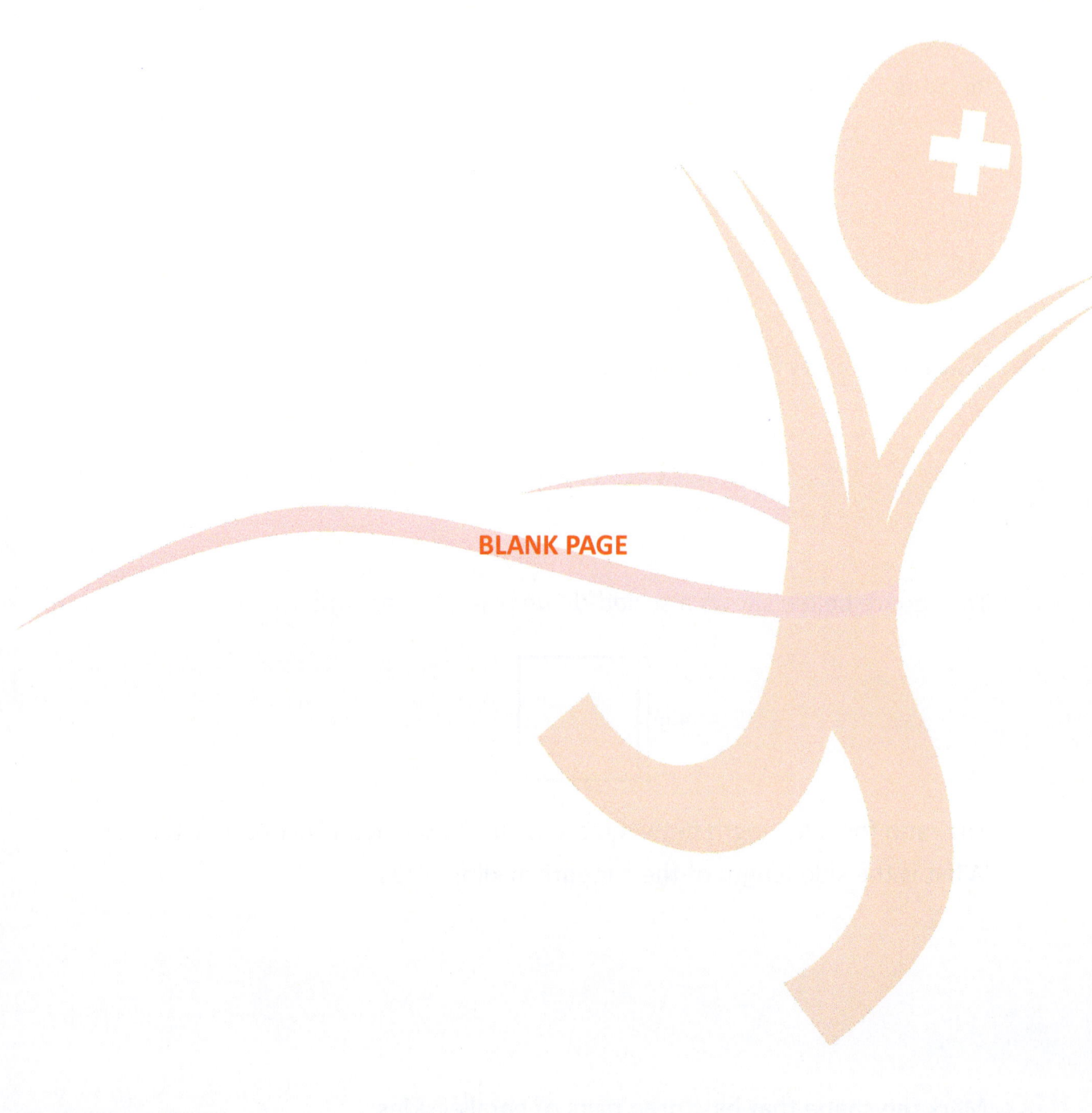

FIRST PAST THE POST

Test 9

6 minutes

Total /20

1. How many of the numbers below are prime?

   1   5   17   27   32   11   23

2. The diagram shows a rectangular-shaped 3D tank partially filled with water. What volume of the tank is occupied by water?

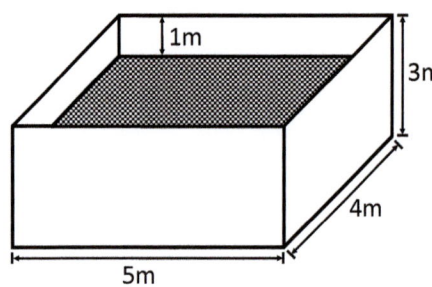

(Diagram not to scale)

 m³

3. An isosceles triangle has base-corner coordinates (3, 1) and (5, 1). What is the x-value of the top-corner coordinates?

4. The clock below shows the time one afternoon and is 1 hour and 15 minutes fast. What is the correct time in 24-hour clock format?

5. What is 1.07km + 130m + 80cm expressed in metres (m)?

 m

6. What is 25% of 50 added to 20% of 80?

7. Round 17.036 to two decimal places.

8. What is the mass indicated by the arrow on the scale below?

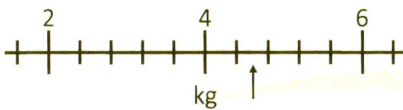

9. What is the next number in the sequence below?

-2   3   10   19   30   43

10. Point P is at (3, -4) and is reflected in the x-axis to form point Q. What are the coordinates of Q?

11. What is the value of $^2/_3 + (^5/_3 \times ^1/_2)$ expressed as an improper fraction in its lowest terms?

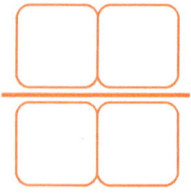

12. The partially completed table below shows the number of children that scored over 70% in a spelling test. How many children scored over 70%?

Class	Tally	Total
1										
2																	
3								7
4											

13. Zak is x years old. The age of his sister is $x - 3$ and his brother's age is $x + 7$. If the sum of their ages is 28 years, how old is Zak?

14. The lengths of 6 out of 7 tree branches are shown in the bar chart below. If the average length of the 7 branches is 60cm, what is the length of branch 5?

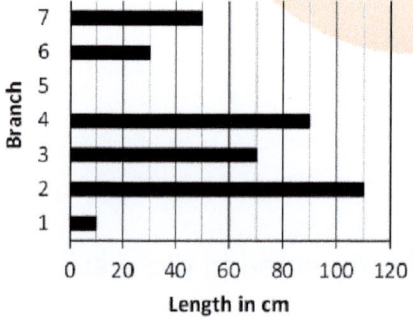

 cm

15. What is the value of 476 - 183?

16. Fabia has 17 bags of change. Seven bags each contain fourteen 50p coins and the remaining 10 bags each contain twenty 10p coins. How much money has Fabia got in change altogether?

£ ☐☐ . ☐☐

17. What are the names of the two 2D shapes A and B? Mark your answer below.

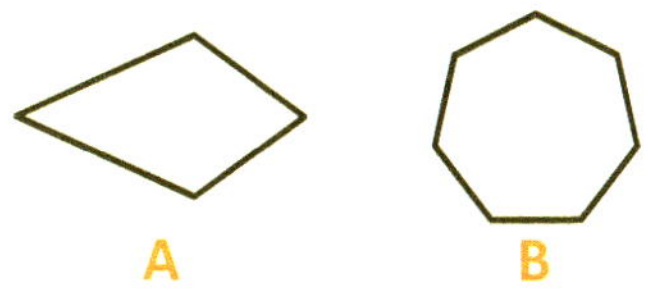

A   B

A. trapezium
B. nonagon

A. kite
B. heptagon

A. hexagon
B. kite

18. Amit is facing northwest (NW) and turns to face exactly in the opposite direction. Which direction is Amit now facing?

19. What is the result of subtracting the perimeter of the rhombus from the perimeter of the equilateral triangle shown below?

(Diagrams not to scale)

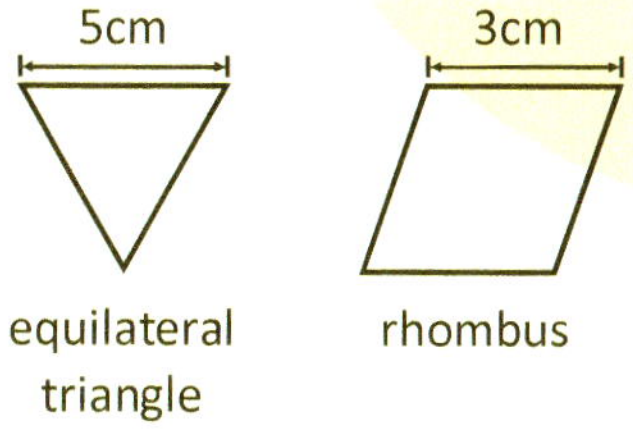

5cm — equilateral triangle
3cm — rhombus

☐☐ cm

20. Four kings and four jacks are removed from a complete deck of 52 cards. What is the probability of picking an ace at random from the remaining cards in the pack? Express your answer in its lowest terms.

☐☐ / ☐☐

Test 10

 6 minutes

Total /20

1. In the following statements 'odd' and 'even' refer to positive whole numbers. Mark the statement that is **false**.

   odd + odd = even ⬭   odd × even = odd ⬭   odd + even = odd ⬭   even × even = even ⬭

2. The distance between Adrian's eyes is 2.3cm to one decimal place. What is the maximum value that this distance could be to two decimal places?

    cm

3. Mark the missing conversions given by the question marks.

   $? = 0.375 = 37.5\%$

   $^9/_{10} = ? = 90\%$

   $^5/_4 = 1.25 = ?$

   $^3/_{16}$, 0.9, 12.5% ⬭ $^2/_5$, 0.89, 125% ⬭ $^3/_8$, 0.9, 125% ⬭

4. Write down the letter of the shape below which has a number of sides that is prime.

5. The numbers 277 and 400 are multiplied together and the result is divided by 50. What is the answer?

6. Write down (as a number) how much the middle digit is worth in the result of 59 + 76.

7. A sequence starts $a, a, ...$ and the third term is the sum of the first two terms. The fourth term is the sum of the second and third terms and so on. Mark the correct expression for the 10th term.

8. The network below shows the roads connecting four landmarks A, B, C and D. Giving your answer in metres, what is the length of the shortest route from A to C?

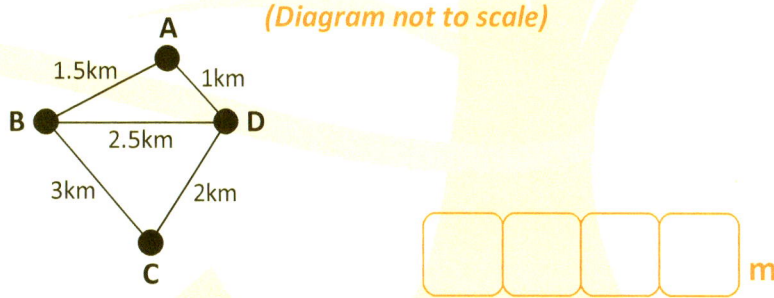 m

9. The point (-4, 0) is reflected in the x-axis. What will be the coordinates of this point after the transformation?

10. What prime factor do the numbers 35 and 42 share?

11. The bar chart below shows the stock of certain goods in a Middle Ages storehouse:

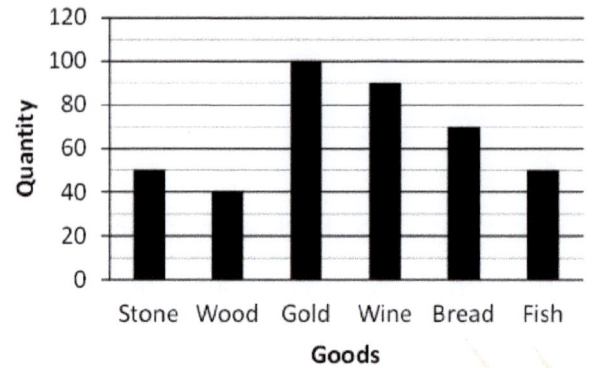

Mark the goods type that is equal to stone in terms of quantity.

Gold ▢   Wine ▢   Bread ▢   Fish ▢   Wood ▢

12. Evaluate s in the formula:

$$s = 1^{30} + 1 - \sqrt{4}$$

13. Solve the equation below, where t represents the price of a laptop computer.

$$75 = (3/8) \times t$$

£ ▢▢

14. Express the ratio 80:64 in its lowest terms.

▢▢ : ▢▢

15. A vertical line crosses the line AB at its centre. The coordinates of A and B are (-7, 3) and (1, 3) respectively. What are the coordinates of the point where the two lines cross?

(▢▢ , ▢▢)

16. A set of toy blocks are numbered 1 to 30 and Jenna picks one up at random. What are the chances that the block has a number on it that is square, cube and triangular?

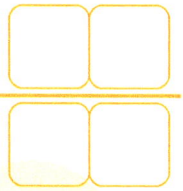

17. Mark the 3D shape with the most combined number of edges and vertices.

18. Consider the diagram below of a small door set into a wall:

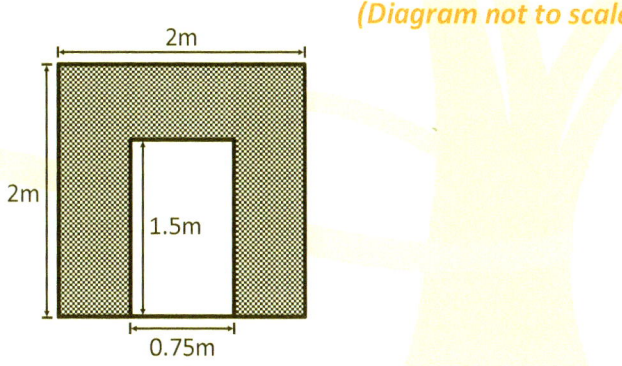

What is the area of the shaded wall region?

 m²

19. Relative to a lighthouse, a ship is to the northeast (NE). Determine the direction of the lighthouse from the ship.

20. Calculate the value of 9,999 - 1,234.5.

BLANK PAGE

FIRST PAST THE POST®

Answers & Explanations

Numerical Reasoning: Quick-Fire

Standard Format

Book 2

Test 1, pages 1-6

Question	Answer	Explanation
1	12	Using BIDMAS: $1{,}000 \times 0.084 = 84$; $84 \div 7 = 12$
2	3	Add five to both sides of the equation to give $12s - 5 + 5 = 31 + 5$ which reduces to $12s = 36$. Dividing both sides by 12 gives $12s \div 12 = 36 \div 12$. Therefore, $s = 36 \div 12 = 3$.
3	-3	The sequence increases from left to right in steps of three. As the first term is missing, its value must be a count of three back from the second term value of 0. Therefore, first term is -3.
4	5	A square-based pyramid has four vertices on the base and one on the top, i.e. five (5) in total.
5	$2/5$	Probability = number of ways of achieving success (2) ÷ total number of possible outcomes (5). Two of the five cards shown are aces. Therefore, the probability of picking an ace is $2/5$.
6	400	The 4 is in the hundreds column and therefore represents 400.
7	5.75	Dividing 3 by 4 in the fraction $3/4$ gives 0.75. Therefore, $5\,3/4 = 5.75$ as a decimal number.
8	(4, 3)	The fourth corner is at the top right of the rectangle. As the bottom-left corner has coordinates (0, 0), the fourth corner's coordinates must be (4, 3) in order to be horizontally in line with corner (0, 3) and vertically above corner (4, 0).
9	6cm²	First convert 60mm to cm; 60mm = 60 ÷ 10 = 6cm Area of triangle = (base × perpendicular height) ÷ 2 = (6 × 2) ÷ 2 = 12 ÷ 2 = 6cm²
10	216	Output = $6^3 = 6 \times 6 \times 6 = 216$
11	4	First, rewrite the numbers in ascending order: 1, 2, **3**, **5**, 7, 8 As there are an even number of values, the median is the mean of the middle two numbers: $(3 + 5) \div 2 = 8 \div 2 = 4$
12	2	A parallelogram maps onto itself twice when rotated through 360° about its centre. The order of rotational symmetry is therefore two (2).
13	160	Using BIDMAS: $28 - 12 = 16$; $3^2 + 1 = 9 + 1 = 10$; $16 \times 10 = 160$
14	90	Red sector percentage = 100% - (40% + 20% + 25%) = 100% - 85% = 15% 15% of 600 = (15 ÷ 100) × 600 = 0.15 × 600 = 90
15	4:3	Dividing each of the ratio parts by a common number results in an equivalent ratio. In this case, dividing by 12 gives 4:3.
16	40%	There are 20 squares in the whole grid, eight of which are shaded (six whole and four halves). The percentage that are shaded = (8 ÷ 20) × 100 = 0.4 × 100 = 40%
17	58cm	Length of tube before cutting = 1m 16cm = 100cm + 16cm = 116cm Length of each tube piece after cutting = 116cm ÷ 2 = 58cm
18	45°	Note that the base and height of the right-angled triangle are both the same length. This is an isosceles right-angled triangle. Therefore, two of the angles must be equal. As angles in a triangle equal 180° and one of the angles is 90°, the other two must each be (180° - 90°) ÷ 2 = 90° ÷ 2 = 45°. Angle $p°$ must therefore be 45°.
19	15:45	15 minutes before 4 o'clock in the afternoon is 3.45pm. To write this in 24–hour format, add 12 hours for pm time, i.e. 15:45.
20	12	Multiples of 4 are 4, 8, **12**, 16, 20, 24 and multiples of 6 are 6, **12**, 18, 24.

Test 2, pages 7-12

Question	Answer	Explanation
1	3	When $y = 5$, $5 = 5(x - 2)$. Divide both sides by 5 to give $1 = x - 2$. Add 2 to both sides to give $x = 3$.
2	816	Using a long multiplication method: $51 \times 16 = 816$
3	282 years	Use subtraction to find the interval: $1348 - 1066 = 282$ years
4	600mm^3	Volume of prism = cross-sectional area × length = $120 \times 5 = 600$mm^3
5	1,850	Number of stone bricks for three houses = $350 \times 3 = 1,050$. Number of stone bricks for two estates = $400 \times 2 = 800$. Total number of stone bricks required = $1,050 + 800 = 1,850$.
6	2 thousandths	The 2 is in the thousandths column and therefore worth 2 thousandths.
7	$1\,{}^3/_{10}$	The lowest common multiple (LCM) of 5 and 2 is 10. Convert both fractions so that their denominators are 10. The sum becomes ${}^{18}/_{10} - {}^5/_{10} = {}^{13}/_{10}$. 10 divides into 13 once with 3 left over so as a mixed number this is $1\,{}^3/_{10}$.
8	false	2 is the largest number that will divide exactly into 18, 32 and 40.
9	13	Counting the dots in the first three terms gives the sequence: 4, 7, 10. The next term in the sequence is found by adding three to the previous term. This means that the fourth term is found by adding three to 10 (the third term) and hence 13 dots are required.
10	2.718	As the fourth decimal digit (2) is less than 5, the third decimal digit (8) stays the same. Therefore, 2.718281 to three decimal places is 2.718.
11	XXVIII	$10 = X$, $5 = V$ and $1 = I$ in Roman numerals. The number 28 consists of 2 tens (XX), 1 five (V) and 3 ones (III), this is XXVIII.
12	square root input	The square root of 144 is 12 as $12 \times 12 = 144$.
13	£13.50	50% of £9.00 = ${}^{50}/_{100} \times £9.00 = £4.50$. Add on to what Bella already has: £9.00 + £4.50 = £13.50
14	cylinder	From the available 3D shapes, only a cylinder has two circular faces.
15	44	Add up each part of the ratio: $5 + 4 + 3 = 12$. Divide the total number of books by 12: $132 \div 12 = 11$. Multiply by the part representing chemistry: $11 \times 4 = 44$ books
16	27	Range = highest value - lowest value = $91 - 64 = 27$
17	${}^5/_{14}$	Total number of balls in the bag = $5 + 9 = 14$. Since five of them are red, the probability of selecting a red ball is ${}^5/_{14}$.
18	24mm	Each subdivision on the ruler is 0.1cm. The arrow on the ruler is pointing four subdivisions after 2cm = $2 + (4 \times 0.1$cm$) = 2$cm $+ 0.4$cm $= 2.4$cm. Convert to millimetres by multiplying by 10: $2.4 \times 10 = 24$mm
19	47°	Angles in a triangle add up to 180°. Third angle = 180° - 91° - 42° = 47°
20	$3x + 14$	The perimeter of the shape = $x + x + x + 7 + 7 = 3x + 14$

Test 3, pages 13-18

Question	Answer	Explanation
1	£7.85	Change = £20.00 - (£8.40 + £3.75) = £20.00 - £12.15 = £7.85.
2	1.7kg	Each subdivision on the scale is worth 0.05kg. The arrow is pointing four subdivisions after 1.5kg. Therefore, the reading = 1.5kg + (4 × 0.05kg) = 1.5kg + 0.2kg = 1.7kg.
3	CXXIX	$5^3 + 2^2 = 125 + 4 = 129$. In Roman numerals, C = 100, X = 10 and IX = 9. 129 = 100 + 10 + 10 + 9 = CXXIX in Roman numerals
4	$1\frac{1}{4}$	First, express $\frac{5}{6}$ in terms of twelfths by multiplying top and bottom by 2 to give $\frac{10}{12}$. $\frac{10}{12} + \frac{5}{12} = \frac{15}{12} = \frac{5}{4}$ (after dividing top and bottom by 3). $\frac{5}{4} = 1\frac{1}{4}$.
5	S	There are 45° between any two directions on the compass. A person turning clockwise from NW 225° has to turn 225 ÷ 45° = 5 steps so comes to rest facing south (S).
6	8	Adding the number of parallel sides on all shapes in order gives: 2 (parallelogram) + 0 (regular pentagon) + 3 (regular hexagon) + 2 (square) + 0 (kite) + 1 (trapezium) + 0 (triangle) = 8.
7	30cm³	The wedge is half the volume of a cuboid with the same dimensions shown. Therefore, volume $(v) = (l \times w \times h) \div 2 = (5 \times 4 \times 3) \div 2 = 60 \div 2 = 30cm^3$.
8	(2, 2)	Rotating point P from (-2, 2) clockwise through 90° about (0, 0) moves P from the top left to the top right quadrant. The y-coordinate remains the same but the x-coordinate changes from -2 to 2. Therefore, the new coordinates P are (2, 2).
9	2	A rhombus is a special type of parallelogram with 4 equal length sides and 2 pairs of parallel sides. It maps onto itself twice when rotated through 360°. Therefore, the answer is 2.
10	14	11 children go to karate only. 3 more belong to both clubs. Total number attending the karate club = 11 + 3 = 14.
11	1, 3, 5, 15	1, 3, 5 and 15 are the only whole numbers that will divide exactly into 15 and therefore are factors of 15.
12	3	Mean = sum of values ÷ number of values = (1 + 4 + 3 + 1 + 4 + 5) ÷ 6 = 18 ÷ 6 = 3.
13	750ml	The scale is in litres and the water level is halfway between 0.5 and 1.0, i.e. 0.75 litres. 0.75 litres × 1,000 = 750ml
14	Friday	February has 29 days in a leap year. As the 25th is a Friday, the 29th must be the following Tuesday and three days into March takes us again to a Friday.
15	12.6cm	A regular nonagon has nine equal length sides. As one side measures 14mm, the shape's perimeter must be 9 × 14mm = 126mm. Divide by 10 to convert to cm, i.e. 126 ÷ 10 = 12.6cm.
16	30	60% of 50 = (60 ÷ 100) × 50 = 0.6 × 50 = 30 questions correct
17	$\frac{1}{36}$	There is a 1 in 6 chance of scoring a three on a single fair die. The probability of scoring a double three on both dice in the same throw is therefore $(\frac{1}{6}) \times (\frac{1}{6}) = \frac{1}{36}$.
18	55	Substituting the values for r, s and t into the expression $(r + s) \times (r - t)$ gives: $(7 + 4) \times (7 - 2) = 11 \times 5 = 55$
19	B	As the net is folded up around the base, squares A, C, D and E form the four side faces of the cube. B will be the top square.
20	16	The sequence is of descending square numbers counting down from 49 to 1. Therefore, the square number missing is 16.

Test 4, pages 19-24

Question	Answer	Explanation
1	293	Add up the number of episodes represented by the bars. $60 + 55 + 40 + 50 + 45 + 43 = 293$
2	12	Using BIDMAS: $13 - (5 \times 1 \div 5) = 13 - 1 = 12$
3	37	$4^3 - 3^3 = 64 - 27 = 37$
4	10	A decagon is a 10-sided 2D shape.
5	2, 2, 5, 5	The prime factors of 100 can be found by writing $100 = 2 \times 50 = 2 \times 2 \times 25 = 2 \times 2 \times 5 \times 5$. Multiplying the prime factors together should give $2 \times 2 \times 5 \times 5 = 100$.
6	$^{15}/_8$	Write $300 \div 160$ as $^{300}/_{160}$. Simplify the fraction by dividing through by 20: $^{300}/_{160} = {}^{15}/_8$.
7	4	The plus shape has four lines of reflective symmetry (one horizontal, one vertical and two diagonal).
8	7	Since the sum of the first four terms is 70: $n + 2n + 3n + 4n = 70$; $10n = 70$ and $n = 7$.
9	2 thousands 0 units	The 2 is in the thousands column and the underlined 0 is in the units column.
10	(3, 3)	The midpoint of the line AB is halfway along both the x-coordinates and y-coordinates. The midpoint of the x-coordinates is $(6 - 0) \div 2 = 6 \div 2 = 3$. Similarly, the midpoint of the y-coordinates is $(6 - 0) \div 2 = 6 \div 2 = 3$. The coordinates of the midpoint are (3, 3).
11	A car's speed will exceed 10,000mph.	It is likely that it will rain for two days in London, and it is likely that an earthquake will occur somewhere in the world. However, a car could never move at 10,000mph so this is an impossible event.
12	27	Using BIDMAS: $(9 \times 12) \div 4 = 108 \div 4 = 27$
13	(3, 5)	Imagine rotating shape ABCD 270° anticlockwise about point D back to its original position. Point B will have coordinates (3, 5).
14	21	Divide the total weight that the lift can hold by the weight of an average person: $1{,}680\text{kg} \div 80\text{kg} = 21$ people
15	0.8m³	Convert 40cm to metres: $40 \div 100 = 0.4$m. Volume of column $= 0.4 \times 0.4 \times 5 = 0.8\text{m}^3$
16	-4	$3 \times 2p + 8 = 4p$; $6p + 8 = 4p$; $6p - 4p = -8$; $2p = -8$; $p = -4$
17	60%	The word ANTITHESIS has 10 letters and six of them are consonants. Write this as $^6/_{10}$ and multiply by 100 to get 60%.
18	0.76	Using BIDMAS: $1.2 - (44 \div 100) = 1.2 - 0.44 = 0.76$
19	12	A cuboid has eight vertices and a tetrahedron has four vertices. Therefore, the combined number of vertices = 8 + 4 = 12.
20	17:45	The time on the clock is 5.45pm. To write this in 24-hour format, add 12 hours for pm time, i.e. 17:45.

Test 5, pages 25-30

Question	Answer	Explanation
1	57,100	57,083 has a 0 in the hundreds column. As the digit in the tens column (8) is larger than 5, the 83 is rounded up to 100 to make 57,100.
2	40	Houses sold in July on the pictogram = $2\ ^3/_4$. Houses sold in August on the pictogram = $2\ ^1/_4$. Total houses sold on the pictogram = $2\ ^3/_4 + 2\ ^1/_4 = 5$. If one house on the pictogram equals eight actual houses then total houses built = $5 \times 8 = 40$.
3	$10,000 cm^2$	Imagine a square with each of its sides 1m in length; its area is $1m \times 1m = 1m^2$. As 1m = 100cm, equivalent area in cm = $100cm \times 100cm = 10,000cm^2$.
4	£26.75	$11 \times £2.05 = £22.55$ and $4 \times 1.05 = £4.20$. Total cost = $£22.55 + £4.20 = £26.75$
5	$^1/_4$	As the spinner is fair, it is equally likely to land on any one of the eight sections. Two of the sections are white, so the probability of landing on a white section = $^2/_8 = ^1/_4$.
6	84	Apply the rule to the last known term of 30 to find the next term. Next term = $30 - 2 = 28$; $28 \times 3 = 84$
7	7	Work backwards from the output applying the inverse number operations in order. $26 - 5 = 21$; $^{21}/_3 = 7$
8	$3d + 50$	At £3 per mile the cost of travelling d miles is $3d$. There is also an additional £50 fixed fee. Therefore, total cost in pounds (£) = $3d + 50$
9	(5, 8)	All points on a vertical line have the same x-coordinate, it is only the y-coordinate that changes. The y-coordinate of the top end must be > 3, so the only possible option is (5, 8).
10	18mm	Each small division on the ruler represent 1mm. The arrow points to two small divisions before 20mm (2cm). Therefore, the answer is 18mm.
11	21	Value of one ratio part = $84 \div (3 + 1) = 84 \div 4 = 21$. Sharing equal parts according to the ratio, number that are **not** blue = $21 \times 1 = 21$.
12	£120	By reading the graph, it can be deduced that one hour = £40, two hours = £60, three hours = £80, four hours = £100. The difference between each hour is £20, so five hours = £100 + £20 = £120.
13	4cm	All dimensions of a cube are the same (l), so we have $l \times l \times l = 64cm^3$. Therefore, $l = \sqrt[3]{64} = 4cm$.
14	(5, 1)	Moving 5 units to the right from (0, 2) moves the corner to (5, 2) i.e. x-coordinate change. Moving 1 unit down from (5, 2) finishes at (5, 1) i.e. y-coordinate change.
15	11	Shape A (square-based pyramid) has 8 edges, shape B (pentagonal prism) has 15 edges and shape C (cuboid) has 12 edges. Therefore, (8 + 15) - 12 = 23 - 12 = 11.
16	4	The mode is the number that occurs most frequently in the set, in this case 4.
17	2 and 7	Note that line 2 slopes left at 45° and line 7 slopes right at 45°. The angle between them is therefore 90° i.e. lines are at right angles.
18	15	As 40% of the children are girls, the remaining 60% must be boys. 60% of 25 children = $(60 \div 100) \times 25 = 0.6 \times 25 = 15$
19	$20m^2$	Length AB = 7m; EF is 1m inside from each edge = 7m - 1m - 1m = 5m. Width AD = 6m; EH is 1m inside from each edge = 6m - 1m - 1m = 4m. Area of pool = $5m \times 4m = 20m^2$
20	kite	From the options available, only a kite has the properties given.

Test 6, pages 31-36

Question	Answer	Explanation
1	$2/9$	First six square numbers (1, 4, 9, 16, 25, 36) contain no numbers divisible by 10. First six triangular numbers (1, 3, 6, **10**, 15, 21) contain one number divisible by 10. **10**, **20** and **30** are also divisible by 10. Therefore, the probability of picking a number that is divisible by 10 = $4/18$ which reduces to $2/9$.
2	P (3, 5) Q (-5, -5)	The coordinates of point P lie three units along the positive x-axis and five units up the positive y-axis i.e. (3, 5). The coordinates of point Q lie five units along the negative x-axis and five units down the negative y-axis i.e. (-5, -5).
3	239	Using BIDMAS: 720 - (169 + 234 + 78) = 720 - 481 = 239.
4	125	Sum of ratio parts = 1 + 2 + 2 + 5 = 10. Divide this by total quantity (250) to get 25. Multiply the largest ratio part (5) by 25 to get 125.
5	2,009,004.7	Convert each word into its number equivalent: two million = 2,000,000; nine thousand = 9,000; four = 4; point seven = 0.7. Aligning them to the correct place values gives 2,009,004.7.
6	248mm	Difference in height: 178.5cm - 153.7cm = 24.8cm. In millimetres: 24.8 × 10 = 248mm.
7	obtuse	An angle of 144° lies between 90° and 180°. Therefore, it is an obtuse angle.
8	34m^2	Rotate and reposition the triangle on the right under the triangle on the left to form a rectangle measuring 15m × 2m. Area to be calculated is now just two rectangles. Total area = (15 × 2) + (4 × 1) = 30 + 4 = 34m^2.
9	57	$11^2 - x = 4^3$; 121 - x = 64; 121 - 64 = x. Therefore, x = 57.
10	120	Using long division, 468 ÷ 4 = 117. To round to the nearest ten, look at the units column, 7 is greater than 5 so the digit in the tens column increases by 1. Therefore, 117 rounds up to 120.
11	$1/16$ and $1/64$	Notice that each term in this sequence is obtained by multiplying the previous one by $1/4$ (or dividing the previous term by 4). The sixth term is $1/4 \times 1/4 = 1/16$ and the seventh term is $1/16 \times 1/4 = 1/64$.
12	6	The first six prime numbers are: 2, 3, **5**, **7**, 11 and 13. Since there are an even number of numbers, the median is the mean of the two middle numbers: (5 + 7) ÷ 2 = 6
13	14	The result of multiplying the input by 0.7 is 0.7t. The output (when t = 20) is 0.7 × 20 = 14.
14	216	A triangle has three sides, an octagon has eight sides and a nonagon has nine sides. Therefore, 3 × 8 × 9 = 216.
15	74 minutes	Phil arrives at West Way at 08:15 and takes 14 minutes before arriving at Sigmund Street at 08:29. He takes 60 minutes before arriving at Rascals Road at 09:29. Total time = 14 + 60 = 74 minutes.
16	350	Percentage of visitors who neither liked nor disliked website = 100% - 88% - 5% = 7%. 7% of 5,000 = (7 ÷ 100) × 5,000 = 0.07 × 5,000 = 350 visitors.
17	(6, -3)	After the reflection P has coordinates (-4, -3). Translating P 10 units to the right gives the final coordinates as (6, -3).
18	100,000ml	A third of 150 = $1/3 \times 150$ = 50. Thus, a reduction by a third is 150 - 50 = 100 litres. In millilitres this is 100 × 1,000 = 100,000ml.
19	3	An equilateral triangle has an order of rotational symmetry of 3. It maps onto itself thrice when rotated through 360° about its centre.
20	$p = r/2 - 3q$	Dividing both sides by two gives $p + 3q = r/2$. Then subtract 3q from both sides: $p = r/2 - 3q$.

Test 7, pages 37-42

Question	Answer	Explanation
1	£1.26	Cost per pencil = 162p ÷ 9 = 18p. 7 × 18p = 126p = £1.26.
2	$4\,5/8$	37 divided into 8 four times (4 × 8 = 32) with $5/8$ remaining i.e. $4 + 5/8 = 4\,5/8$.
3	84	Work backwards from the output applying the inverse number operations in order. Therefore, 12 × 7 = 84.
4	25	The LHS = 28 - 11 + 9 = 26. To balance both sides, the RHS must also equal 26. Therefore, $14 + 37 - x = 26$; $51 - x = 26$; $51 - 26 = x$; $x = 25$.
5	440,000	To round to the nearest 10,000, look at the thousands column. As the digit in the thousands column is 9, which is greater than 5, the 9,728 is rounded up. The ten-thousands column number increases by 1 (from 3 to 4) to give 440,000.
6	21	The HCF of 30, 60 and 75 is 15 and the LCM of 9, 12 and 18 is 36. Difference = 36 - 15 = 21.
7	7	Substituting $y = 25$ into the equation $y = 4x - 3$ gives $25 = 4x - 3$. Therefore, $25 + 3 = 4x$; $28 = 4x$; $28 ÷ 4 = x$; $x = 7$.
8	5	$\sqrt{(3^2 + 4^2)} = \sqrt{(9 + 16)} = \sqrt{25} = 5$.
9	36	This is a sequence of triangular numbers (1, **3**, **6**, **10**, 15, 21, …). Therefore, terms four and five have 15 and 21 circles respectively, a total of 36 circles.
10	0.064	As $0.4 = 4/10$ we can write $0.4 × 0.4 × 0.4$ as $4/10 × 4/10 × 4/10 = 64/1{,}000 = 0.064$.
11	28km per hour	Observe from the graph that distance travelled in 30 minutes is 14km. Therefore, distance travelled in 60 minutes = 2 × 14km = 28km.
12	5cm	The diameter of the largest circle must be 100mm i.e. equal to the width of the square. Radius of circle = diameter ÷ 2 = 100mm ÷ 2 = 50mm. 50mm ÷ 10 = 5cm.
13	118°	Angles on a straight line equal 180°; $n° = 180° - 62° = 118°$.
14	$5/6$	On a die, there are numbers 1 to 6, five of which are greater than or equal to 2. Therefore, the probability of scoring a number greater than or equal to 2 is given by: number of favourable outcomes / total number of outcomes = $5/6$.
15	£72	Value of one ratio part = £360 ÷ (3 + 2) = £72. Sharing equal parts according to the ratio gives: larger share = 3 × £72 = £216, smaller share = 2 × £72 = £144. Difference = £216 - £144 = £72.
16	3	Five 20cm wide tiles will form 1 row across a 1m (100cm) width. 5 rows will cover the 1m² area. Number of tiles = 5 × 5 = 25. Therefore, 28 - 25 = 3 tiles left over.
17	1 square 4 triangles	The net would have 1 square base and 4 triangles which fold up to create the 3D shape.
18	parallelogram	A and B (top two corners) are not horizontally aligned with C and D (bottom two corners) as in a parallelogram. The length and width are not equal therefore it cannot be a rhombus.
19	72mm	The shape is a regular hexagon. Each side length = 2 × 6mm = 12mm. 6 × 12mm = 72mm.
20	09:15	Dario can only take Bus B at 08:55 from the High Street stop; this will get to the Library stop at 09:15.

Test 8, pages 43-48

Question	Answer	Explanation
1	50	Three balls are added and four are taken away from the box every hour. Overall, there is a decrease of one ball per hour. Since there are 50 balls in the box initially, it will take 50 hours for the box to be empty.
2	37°C	The temperatures (from top to bottom) are 29°C and -8°C. Difference = 29 - (-8) = 29 + 8 = 37°C
3	$1/2$	Since A and B are independent events, their probabilities can be multiplied: $3/10 \times q = 3/20$. $q = 3/20 \div 3/10 = 3/20 \times 10/3 = 30/60 = 1/2$
4	3mm	Volume of a cube = $l \times l \times l = l^3$. Since $27 = 3^3$, the length of a side is 3mm.
5	650ml	The jug can hold 1L which is equal to 1,000ml. There are 10 subdivisions in the jug, each representing 1,000 ÷ 10 = 100ml. The level of fruit juice in the jug is 3.5 divisions below 1,000ml which equals 1,000ml - (3.5 x 100ml) = 1,000ml - 350ml = 650ml.
6	4	The largest number that will divide exactly into 20, 44 and 64 is 4, so this is the HCF.
7	$7/20$	Convert $1\ 1/4$ to an improper fraction to get $5/4$. The sum becomes $5/4 - 9/10$. The denominator is the LCM of 4 and 10 which is 20. $(5 \times 5 / 4 \times 5) - (9 \times 2 / 10 \times 2) = 25/20 - 18/20 = 7/20$.
8	Q $(x, y + 3)$ R $(x + 4, y)$	As Q is directly above P their x-coordinates are equal (both x). Similarly, if R is on the same horizontal line as P their y-coordinates are equal (both y). Since PQ is 3 units and PR is 4 units the only possible coordinates from the options given are Q $(x, y + 3)$ and R $(x + 4, y)$.
9	mean < median	Mean = (9 + 18 + 7 + 15 + 16) ÷ 5 = 65 ÷ 5 = 13. Rearrange numbers in ascending order: 7, 9, 15, 16, 18. Middle number (median) is 15. Hence the mean is less than the median.
10	59°	Angles on a straight line add up to 180°. Therefore, internal angle = 180° - 121° = 59°. Using the fact that opposite angles in a parallelogram are equal means that $a° = 59°$.
11	468	Using addition and subtraction: 987 - ? - 519 = 0; 468 - ? = 0; ? = 468
12	5	Substitute values into formula then calculate sum: $4500 = a(1,000 - 10^2)$; $4,500 = a(1,000 - 100)$; $4,500 = 900a$; $4,500 \div 900 = a$ and $a = 5$
13	drawbar	The drawbar sector contains a right-angle (90°). 90° is a quarter of the whole (360°). $1/4$ is equal to 25%.
14	0	When the instruction is to multiply by 0 the output will always be 0 (regardless of input).
15	14.5cm	Perimeter = 3.7 + 2.4 + 2.1 + 3.5 + 2.8 = 14.5cm
16	pentagonal prism	A pentagonal prism has two end faces and five rectangular faces, so seven in total. The others all have an even number of faces: tetrahedron (4), cube (6), cone (2).
17	44	The rest of August (28th to 31st) is four days. There are 30 days in September and a further 10 in October until Rhonda's birthday. So, days between dates is 4 + 30 + 10 = 44 days.
18	2	The capital letter H has 2 lines of reflective symmetry (1 horizontal and 1 vertical).
19	0.1km	The ratio 1cm:25m means that 4cm on the plan represents a side length of 100m on the actual car park. Knowing 1,000m = 1km, divide 100 by 1,000 to get 0.1km.
20	regular hexagon	A regular hexagon has three pairs of parallel sides.

Test 9, pages 49-54

Question	Answer	Explanation
1	4	Prime numbers are numbers that have only two factors, 1 and the number itself. Therefore, there are four numbers in the list which are prime numbers: 5, 17, 11 and 23.
2	40m³	Height (h) of water in tank = 3m - 1m = 2m. Volume = $l \times b \times h$ = 5m × 4m × 2m = 40m³
3	4	The x-coordinate of the top vertex of the isosceles triangle is exactly halfway between the x-coordinates of the two base vertices. Halfway between 3 and 5 is 4.
4	15:15	The time shown on the clock is 4.30pm. As the clock is fast, we must subtract 1 hour and 15 minutes. Subtracting 1 hour gives 3.30pm. Subtracting a further 15 minutes brings the actual time to 3.15pm. We add 12 hours to account for the pm time. This gives 15:15 in 24-hour clock format.
5	1200.8m	First, convert km and cm to metres (m): 1.07km × 1,000 = 1,070m and 80cm ÷ 100 = 0.8m. 1,070m + 130m + 0.8m = 1,200.8m.
6	28.5	25% of 50 = (25 ÷ 100) × 50 = 0.25 × 50 = 12.5; 20% of 80 = (20 ÷ 100) × 80 = 0.2 × 80 = 16. 12.5 + 16 = 28.5.
7	17.04	To round to two decimal places, first look at three decimal places. As the number in the thousandth column (6) is greater than 5, it is rounded up and the hundredth column number increases by 1 (from 3 to 4) to give 17.04 to 2 decimal places.
8	4.6kg	1 large division = 2kg. Each one is split into five small divisions, each worth 2kg ÷ 5 = 0.4kg. Reading indicated by the arrow = 4kg + 0.4kg (one small division) + 0.2kg (half a small division) = 4.6kg.
9	58	Note that the difference between adjacent pair of terms is another sequence of ascending odd numbers starting from 5. The difference between the previous numbers was 43 - 30 = 13. Therefore, the difference between 43 and the next number is 15 so the next number must be 43 + 15 = 58.
10	(3, 4)	As the reflection is in the x-axis, only the y-coordinate value will change. -4 becomes +4. Therefore, the coordinates are (3,4).
11	$3/2$	$2/3 + (5/3 \times 1/2) = 2/3 + 5/6 = 4/6 + 5/6 = 9/6 = 3/2$
12	45	Class 1 tally (9) + Class 2 tally (18) + Class 3 tally (7) + Class 4 tally (11) = 45
13	8	$x + x - 3 + x + 7 = 28; 3x + 4 = 28; 3x = 28 - 4; 3x = 24; x = 24 \div 3 = 8$
14	60cm	Average (60cm) = (10 + 110 + 70 + 90 + ? + 30 + 50) ÷ 7; 60 = (360 + ?) ÷ 7; 60 × 7 = (360 + ?); 420 = (360 + ?); 420 - 360 = ? = 60cm.
15	293	Using a standard column subtraction method, 476 - 183 = 293.
16	£69	The sum is 7(14 × 50p) + 10(20 × 10p) = (7 × £7) + (10 × £2) = £49 + £20 = £69
17	A. kite B. heptagon	Recognise kite for Shape A, and note that Shape B has seven sides indicating a heptagon.
18	SE	To turn and face the opposite direction is to turn through 180°. Opposite direction to NW is SE.
19	3cm	An equilateral triangle has 3 equal length sides and a rhombus has 4 equal length sides. The difference is therefore (3 × 5cm) - (4 × 3cm) = 15cm - 12cm = 3cm.
20	$1/11$	Cards remaining = 52 - 8 = 44. There are 4 aces in a pack, probability of picking an ace = $4/44 = 1/11$.

Test 10, pages 55-60

Question	Answer	Explanation
1	odd × even = odd	The incorrect option is odd × even = odd. Any (whole) number multiplied by an even number is an even number because multiplication is just repeated addition, and adding even numbers yields even numbers. E.g. 3 × 8 = 8 + 8 + 8 = 24 which is even.
2	2.34cm	If the second decimal digit was 5 or more, the first decimal digit (3) would be rounded up. Since this must stay as a 3, the maximum second decimal digit value can only be 4.
3	$^3/_8$, 0.9, 125%	For the first conversion, 0.375 is $^{375}/_{1,000}$ which reduces to $^3/_8$. The second conversion can be found by dividing out the fraction $^9/_{10}$ to get 0.9. The final conversion is obtained by multiplying 1.25 by 100 to get 125%.
4	C	A prime number has only two factors: 1 and itself. Therefore, C is the only shape with a prime number of sides (3).
5	2,216	Divide 400 by 50 to get 8. Using long multiplication: 277 × 8 = 2,216
6	30	59 + 76 = 135. The digit in the tens column is a 3 so it is worth 30.
7	55a	Continuing the sequence using the given rule: a, a, 2a, 3a, 5a, 8a, 13a, 21a, 34a, 55a. The 10th term is 55a.
8	3,000m	There are four routes through the network from A to C. Add up the distances along these routes and compare to find the shortest. This is ADC which is 1 + 2 = 3km. Knowing 1,000m = 1km, in metres this is 3 × 1,000 = 3,000m.
9	(-4, 0)	Note that (-4, 0) lies on the x-axis already, so a reflection in this axis has no effect.
10	7	35 can be written as 5 × 7; 42 is the product of 6 × 7 and the 6 is the product of 2 × 3. So, 35 = 5 × 7 and 42 = 2 × 3 × 7. The common prime factor of 35 and 42 is 7.
11	Fish	The goods type that has the same quantity (50) as stone is fish.
12	0	1 to any power is 1 so 1^{30} is 1. √4 = 2. So, s = 1 + 1 - 2 = 0
13	£200	Multiply both sides by 8 to give 600 = 3t. Dividing through by 3 gives t = £200.
14	5:4	Find the largest number that will divide exactly into both parts of the ratio. This is 16 as 80 ÷ 16 = 5 and 64 ÷ 16 = 4. Hence the reduced ratio is 5:4.
15	(-3, 3)	As A and B have equal y-coordinate values of (3), AB is a horizontal line and the y-coordinate stays the same (3). The vertical line will cross at the midpoint of the x-coordinate values which is (-7 + 1) ÷ 2 = -6 ÷ 2 = -3. Therefore, the coordinates are (-3, 3).
16	$^1/_{30}$	The only block with a number from 1 to 30 that fulfils all three criteria is 1. Therefore the chances of picking this block is $^1/_{30}$.
17	hexagonal prism	The hexagonal prism has 18 edges and 12 vertices. Total number of edges and vertices = 18 + 12 = 30. For square-based pyramid total is 13; for cuboid total is 20.
18	2.875m^2	Area of shaded wall region = area of wall - area of door = (2 × 2) - (1.5 × 0.75) = 4 - 1.125 = 2.875m^2
19	SW	From the ship's point of view, when it is facing the lighthouse it is pointing in a southwest (SW) direction i.e. the opposite direction to NE.
20	8,764.5	Use subtraction method and write 9,999 as 9,999.0 to ensure place values line up. 9,999.0 - 1,234.5 = 8,764.5

Other Titles in the First Past The Post® Series

Numerical Reasoning: Quick-Fire

The numerical reasoning section of most 11 plus and Common Entrance exams contains multi-part questions, which are designed to test the candidate's raw mathematical ability. This series is tailored towards the Centre for Evaluation and Monitoring (CEM) Numerical Reasoning assessments but provides invaluable practice for all exam boards. Each book contains 10 tests, each of which comprises 20 questions and is designed to be completed in six minutes. Full answers and explanations are included. Each book allows access to our Peer-Compare Online system, which assesses the candidate's performance anonymously on a question-by-question basis.

Multiple Choice

Multiple choice books provide the candidate with several options from which to choose when answering each question. This catches some candidates out by giving plausible options alongside the correct answer.

Standard Format

Standard format books do not provide the candidate with any options to choose from when answering; candidates must instead write the answer themselves in the space provided. This is challenging for candidates who rely on a process of elimination when answering multiple choice questions.

Other Titles in the First Past The Post® Series

Numerical Reasoning: Multi-Part

The numerical reasoning section of most 11 plus and Common Entrance exams contains multi-part questions, which require several conclusions to be drawn from the same initial information. This series is tailored towards the Centre for Evaluation and Monitoring (CEM) Numerical Reasoning assessments but provides invaluable practice for all exam boards. Full answers and explanations are included. Each book allows access to our Peer-Compare Online system, which assesses the candidate's performance anonymously on a question-by-question basis.

Multiple Choice

Multiple choice books provide the candidate with several options from which to choose when answering each question. This catches some candidates out by giving plausible options alongside the correct answer. Each book contains 10 tests, each of which comprises six multi-part questions, each with five parts. Each test is designed to be completed in 15 minutes.

Standard Format

Standard format books do not provide the candidate with any options to choose from when answering; candidates must instead write the answer themselves in the space provided. This is challenging for candidates who rely on a process of elimination when answering multiple choice questions. Each book contains 10 tests, each of which comprises five multi-part questions. Each test is designed to be completed in 20 minutes.

Other Titles in the First Past The Post® Series

Mathematics: Dictionary Plus

This book is an indispensable companion to our practice papers and workbooks, containing definitions of key mathematical concepts in accessible language. Each definition is accompanied by a worked, illustrated example and a series of questions to ensure a thorough understanding of its practical applications. The questions have two tiers of difficulty: 'Test yourself' and 'Challenge yourself'. Full answers are included.

This is a comprehensive reference volume, invaluable for all students at 11 plus and Common Entrance exams, Key Stage 2 and beyond.

Kaplan Publishing are constantly finding new ways to make a difference to your studies and our exciting online resources really do offer something different to students looking for exam success.

This book comes with free MyKaplan online resources so that you can study anytime, anywhere. This free online resource is not sold separately and is included in the price of the book.

Having purchased this book, you have access to the following online study materials:

CONTENT	ACCA (including FFA, FAB, FMA)		FIA (excluding FFA, FAB, FMA)	
	Text	Kit	Text	Kit
Electronic version of the book	✓	✓	✓	✓
Check Your Understanding Test with instant answers	✓			
Material updates	✓	✓	✓	✓
Latest official ACCA exam questions*		✓		
Extra question assistance using the signpost icon**		✓		
Timed questions with an online tutor debrief using clock icon***		✓		
Interim assessment including questions and answers	✓		✓	
Technical answers	✓	✓	✓	✓

* Excludes F1, F2, F3, F4, FAB, FMA and FFA; for all other papers includes a selection of questions, as released by ACCA
** For ACCA P1–P7 only
*** Excludes F1, F2, F3, F4, FAB, FMA and FFA

How to access your online resources

Kaplan Financial students will already have a MyKaplan account and these extra resources will be available to you online. You do not need to register again, as this process was completed when you enrolled. If you are having problems accessing online materials, please ask your course administrator.

If you are not studying with Kaplan and did not purchase your book via a Kaplan website, to unlock your extra online resources please go to www.mykaplan.co.uk/addabook (even if you have set up an account and registered books previously). You will then need to enter the ISBN number (on the title page and back cover) and the unique pass key number contained in the scratch panel below to gain access.

You will also be required to enter additional information during this process to set up or confirm your account details.

If you purchased through Kaplan Flexible Learning or via the Kaplan Publishing website you will automatically receive an e-mail invitation to MyKaplan. Please register your details using this email to gain access to your content. If you do not receive the e-mail or book content, please contact Kaplan Publishing.

Your Code and Information

This code can only be used once for the registration of one book online. This registration and your online content will expire when the final sittings for the examinations covered by this book have taken place. Please allow one hour from the time you submit your book details for us to process your request.

Please scratch the film to access your MyKaplan code.

Please be aware that this code is case-sensitive and you will need to include the dashes within the passcode, but not when entering the ISBN. For further technical support, please visit www.MyKaplan.co.uk